Piano Lessons

PIANO LESSONS

A Memoir

Anna Goldsworthy

St. Martin's Press   New York

www.stmartins.com

ISBN 978-0-312-64628-8

First published in Australia by Black Inc., an imprint of Schwartz Media Pty Ltd

First U.S. Edition: October 2010

10   9   8   7   6   5   4   3   2   1

For Eleonora,
and for my two Reubens,
who bookend these memories

Piano Lessons

PART I.

Chapter 1. Bach

I T WAS MY GRANDFATHER WHO FOUND HER. He pronounced her name with an extravagant French accent that spoke of her mystery, her glamour.

Mrs Siv-*an*.

She had recently arrived in Adelaide with her husband and teenage son and was teaching piano at a western-suburbs high school. My grandfather was a regional director of the Education Department, and he had chanced upon one of her lessons during a routine inspection.

'He was true gentleman, of course, very charming,' she told me later, 'but with a natural authority.' She furrowed her brow and pointed her finger: '*You will teach my granddaughter.*'

I was nine years old and learning piano from a local jazz muso. After our lessons, he liked to join my parents in the kitchen, roll strange-smelling cigarettes and talk about Stevie Wonder. My father had for many years resisted my grandfather's natural authority, and saw no reason for this arrangement to change, until one afternoon the jazz muso rolled a cigarette and announced it was time for me to move on.

'She got an A for First Grade, man! Where to from here?'

It was no longer only my grandfather's idea: my father could safely take it up.

'Mrs Sivan is from Russia,' he told me that night at dinner. 'She's on the Liszt list.'

'What's the list list?'

'The *Liszt* list. Liszt taught the teacher of her teacher's teacher.'

'Who's Liszt?'

He gave me one of his looks. 'A *very* famous composer.'

I liked the sound of that. If I learned piano from Mrs Sivan, then I too would be on the Liszt list. It sat well with the grand narrative I had in mind for my life.

A week later, my grandfather drove me to Mrs Sivan's house for the audition; my mother sat beside him wearing her best lavender pant-suit, smelling of Chanel. As we drove down North East Road, he recommended I pay serious attention to directions.

'We now approach Ascot Avenue, elsewhere known as Portrush Road. Here we undertake a right-hand turn.'

This was a journey that would be tracked into my body over the following years, as I made it once a week, then twice a week, and then sometimes every day. But for now, my grandfather might have been taking me on an intergalactic voyage from my suburban Adelaide childhood to somewhere very far away.

'At this point, we arrive at our destination,' he announced, as we pulled up outside a cream-brick bungalow. 'The home of the distinguished Mrs Eleonora Siv-*an*, formerly of the Leningrad Conservatorium of Music.'

At the front door there were courtly nods and handshakes all round, and my grandfather and mother speaking too loudly.

'And how are you enjoying your new house, Mrs Sivan?' my grandfather asked.

'Yes, we like enormous. *Much* more comfortable than Pennington Hostel.'

They all laughed, and I dared look up. How to describe her? In my mind she is less a character than a force. Music is coiled inside her under a pressure that demands expression, and from the moment she opened the door she did not stop talking. She must have been in her forties, but was not much taller than my nine-year-old self, and had the peachy, springy skin of an infant. I met her powerful gaze and blushed and dropped my eyes.

'We are not teaching piano playing,' she said. Her English was new, and I was not sure if I had heard correctly. 'We are teaching philosophy and life and music digested. Music is yours. Instrument is *you are*. Come in, please come in.'

She ushered us into her living room and directed me to an ancient upright piano with yellowing keys.

'Music is logically created fantasy,' she continued. 'When I give information, this information comes to student to digest. When digestion coming, the nutrition is his own – is not mine.'

I scanned the room, searching for something of the known world to which I could anchor myself. The piano was pushed against a wall painted a lurid, metallic pink. In the middle of this wall there was a calendar, and I pinned my hopes on this.

'What is the result of a clever, clever heart, and a very kind and generous brain?'

I stared at my mother, willing her to answer, but she avoided my gaze.

'It is clever hands!' Mrs Sivan declared.

'Indeed it is,' said my grandfather. 'Now, I imagine you would like to hear Anna play her Mozart sonata.'

'Of course. Please, make yourself comfortable. Always think first of music, and not to impress us. And never start until you are ready. This is first arts of any music: learn to listen to silence, atmospheric silence. Only then can we understand future and perspective.'

'Where should I begin?' My voice was very small.

'What?'

My father had urged me to begin with the slow movement, because I played it 'very musically'. 'Should I begin with the second movement?'

She looked shocked. 'Always best to start story from beginning, yes? Of course must be first movement.'

At this stage, I viewed piano pieces as obstacle courses for fingers, in which the object was getting through to the end, largely unscathed. The first movement of the Mozart sonata was a hazardous place, but I dodged a few accidentals in the development section and made it to the double barline.

There was silence. I looked at my mother, who looked at my grandfather, who looked at Mrs Sivan.

'Thank you,' she said, finally. 'You like chocolate, yes? Come with me, and I give *wonderful* chocolate.'

My mother nodded encouragingly, and I followed Mrs Sivan out to the kitchen, where she gave me a Baci chocolate, wrapped in silver foil, and then another, and then two more. 'You are good girl, and now must enjoy your life.' She called in her teenage son, Dmitri, to sit with me, and returned to the lounge room to speak to my mother and grandfather.

I looked around the room as my heart beat wildly in my chest. There were framed photographs of dogs on the walls, dressed in spectacles and hats.

'Who took these photos?' I asked Dmitri. He had dark hair and gentle eyes.

'My uncle.' He named the dogs, one by one.

'Do you come from Russia?'

'Yes.'

I had no further small talk, so I munched through my hoard of chocolate in silence.

Eventually, Mrs Sivan collected me. 'I give you kiss,' she said. 'Nine-year-old girl who tries so hard. Of course you must be allowed to learn. But always remember, sounds themselves are emotional response and reflection of contents of your heart and mind. Music is not just playing right notes in right time, but *digestion* hugely important. Enormous job really, but so rewarding, and so makes it worth to live!'

There was a festive atmosphere in the car on the way home.

'Fancy that!' said my mother. 'My clever baby.'

'My dear, you are to be commended on making such a fine impression,' my grandfather declared.

Later, Mrs Sivan explained that she had taken pity on me. That any child who laboured through a Mozart sonata, so ill-equipped, deserved to be taught.

'Her acceptance is not without conditions,' my grandfather continued. 'Mrs Sivan expects you to practise more. Two hours a day. But not all at once. Forty minutes before school, forty minutes in the afternoon and forty minutes in the evening.'

Two hours a day. It sounded catastrophic, but also thrilling.

The jazz muso had asked me to practise for five minutes every day.

Five minutes every single day? For the rest of my life until I died? I was not sure that I could make such a commitment.

'You find time to brush your teeth every day,' he said, but even that seemed a barely endurable ordeal. He never enforced this practice regime, but had a *laissez-faire* approach to teaching, humming quietly while I played, occasionally pencilling in a remark on my music: *Dynamics.* Once he told me not to move my bum up the piano seat to reach a high note. *Bum.* I giggled to hear the word.

The most passionate I ever saw him was when my father told him I hated Stevie Wonder's 'Lately'. 'How could you hate "Lately"?' he asked. His hippy eyes widened; his head shook to a disbelieving slo-mo beat. 'Wow. It's such a beautiful song.'

I could not explain why I hated 'Lately' any more than I could explain why I hated milk, or trains, or the wood shop. There was something about its chromaticism that bothered me, something unsettling about the way my father crooned it, late at night, at the piano: *Lately I've been havin' the strangest feelings with no vivid reason here to find.*

'I just hate it. It's yuck,' I said.

As a six-year-old, the first piece I had loved was an anonymous gigue from the Australian Music Examinations Board Preliminary book. At the climax, it detoured briefly into the secondary dominant, as I would later learn. There was a piquancy to this, as B flat yielded to B natural and then reasserted itself. It was the piece's sweet spot: a rudimentary version of what George Sand called Chopin's 'blue note'. I played these two bars over and over again; I wanted to rub them into my skin. After too many repetitions, they lost their magic, and I had to return to the piece's beginning to recharge them.

One Sunday lunch at my grandparents' house, the men retreated to the music room for their weekly Chopin play-off. My grandfather began with a sprightly waltz, my father played the polonaise that was my bedtime lullaby, and then my uncle trumped them both with the *Fantasie-Impromptu*.

'Bravo,' applauded my grandfather.

'My *smarter younger brother!*' my father cried out, jumping up from his seat. 'Now kiss the carpet!'

As they wrestled, I slipped onto the piano stool and performed my gigue, hoping to silence them.

'That's lovely, darling,' my grandmother said, bringing in the tea.

'We really have to consider a more serious teacher,' my grandfather declared, missing the point entirely.

❄

When we returned home from the audition, I phoned my father at the surgery to tell him the good news.

'Excellent work, Pie! What did you play?'

I confessed that I had only played the first movement, and there was a disappointed silence at the other end of the line. 'Imagine the impression you would have made with the slow movement!' he muttered, finally.

My first lesson with Mrs Sivan was scheduled for the following week, and to please my father I brought along the second movement. Now that I had passed the audition, I felt more confident: the hard work was done. I put the music on the stand and positioned my hands over a G-major chord.

'Not!' she called out. 'Stop!'

'But I haven't even started.'

'Of course music has started already!' She reached over and took my hand. 'The fingers are the orchestral musicians. The elbow must be here, for to conduct. We must hear the sound *before*, and then *immediately* we relax.'

As she demonstrated a chromatic scale, her hand had the grace of a small animal.

'I am relaxed,' I insisted, and imitated her, but my little finger stuck up vertically, an incriminating, impertinent erection.

'Not. You are playing. Not listening.'

This was something she repeated for years before I started to understand it. It is only by hearing a sound first in your imagination that you relax. And it is only by relaxing that you properly hear that sound, be mindful of that sound, understand it as a sound in time, in context of a past and future.

'Not. Not like this. This is *spaghetti fingers*.'

As I played, I skated across the top of the keyboard, but now she took my fingers and introduced them to the bottom of the keys, so that I felt the security of gravity, of contact with the earth. 'Here, feel the depths.' Slowly I would learn to live here, transferring these safe depths from sound to sound, avoiding spillage.

'You must have strong fingers!' She burrowed her fingertips into the top of my arm, so that I almost fell off the stool. 'My darling, I am sorry! I forget my strength.' She laughed. 'Always remember, your hands must speak. Your hand and your instrument are one, not two, and your music inside of you.'

Somehow, over the years that followed, she transferred a physical knowledge from her hands to mine. You do not consciously mould your hands into sounds, any more than you consciously shape your mouth to form a word. You put them on the instrument, and you speak.

'Every note is important,' she said, 'every sound says something.'

I examined the score warily, wondering what this F sharp said, what the meaning of this embellishment might be.

'Every piece tells a story,' she concluded. 'Next week I want you to tell me story of this second movement.'

Back at home, I placed the Mozart score on the kitchen bench and stared miserably at the second movement, waiting for it to talk to me.

'What sort of story?' I asked my mother, as she prepared a stir-fry.

'You're good at stories. Why don't you just make one up?'

'Like what?' I asked.

She stopped slicing vegetables and came over to look at the score. 'I don't know. A little girl goes to the zoo, or something.'

So I invented a story, and grafted it onto the movement. Here a little girl buys some fairy floss; here she sits in the rotunda; at the reprise, she meets a rhinoceros.

What did music mean to me at this time, when I knew nothing of it, when it was a language I did not yet speak? My dream was to be a singer, and I spent much of my spare time singing 'You Light Up My Life' in the study, twirling dramatically between verses, while my father accompanied me on piano. There was an older girl at my primary school, Erica, with a beautiful voice. How marvellous to be able to sing like that! Better than having supernatural powers! Much of my fantasy life involved Erica and me and Tiny Tina and Little Joey from *Young Talent Time*, dressed in flowing white robes, singing on a revolving stage under a disco ball. We looked like angels; sometimes we even were.

At carols night at school, Erica sang 'The Little Drummer Boy'. 'Do you think I'll ever be able to sing like that?' I asked my mother on the way home, with a false, preening modesty.

She thought for a moment.

'No, darling, I don't think you will.'

For the rest of the car trip, I sat in shocked silence. That was not what a mother was supposed to say.

I tried again a few weeks later. 'Do you think I'll ever go on *Young Talent Time*?' I asked my parents as they watched the evening news. Perhaps if I caught them off-guard, they would give me the response I required.

They exchanged uncertain glances.

'Maybe if you practise the piano really hard,' my father offered.

My brother and I had a babysitter who claimed to play the 'Moonlight' Sonata. In her interpretation, she transposed the first movement into E minor, forsook the left hand and soprano voice, and removed all harmonic progression, until the movement was reduced to an E-minor broken chord in second inversion, repeated indefinitely.

'Do you want to hear "Moonlight" Sonata?' I asked visitors, in preparation for *Young Talent Time*. I played this broken chord over and over again, faster and faster, my hand cramped in a spasm of effort. *B—E—G, B—E—G, B-E-G, BEG, BEG-BEGBEGBEG.*

'The "Moonlight" Sonata is a cinch,' I said modestly. 'It's just *B-E-G*, or in other words *beg*.'

This was my knowledge base. This was what I took to my first lessons with Mrs Sivan. At the Leningrad Conservatorium, she had been preparing students for international competitions; before coming to Adelaide, she had never taught children. During our second lesson, I began telling her my story about the zoo.

'This is where the little girl sees a chimpanzee,' I said, pointing to a chromatic embellishment. My voice faltered. Even I did not believe it.

She took my hand: 'My darling, we must sit and work.'

❈

After my first few lessons, my parents swapped shifts at their doctors' surgery so that my father could take me to Mrs Sivan's house. For the next eight years, he accompanied me to my lessons every Tuesday afternoon, listening, day-dreaming, taking notes. Mrs Sivan was a born performer, and enjoyed having him there. I feel it myself now as a teacher: the extra voltage an audience lends to a room.

'Let us talk about the fingers,' Mrs Sivan said. 'This finger, the pointer finger, is good student. This third finger, it is very – what you say – reliable. But this finger … oy.' She shook her head. 'Fourth finger *very* lazy!'

Her words were picturesque but to me entirely abstract. Over the years, my body came to understand them for me.

'It is the thumb that makes a pianist,' she said, and showed me what the thumb can do, her hands fluttering over the keyboard, kneading at it, producing sounds of striking intensity. Over time, I learnt that the thumb is the key to the hand's relaxation, its checkpoint, navigator and conductor. There is an instinct to grab with the thumb, which turns it into a brake; pianistic fluency depends on letting it go, on trusting the hand.

Then she took my little finger into her hand: 'It is the little finger that makes an artist.' She winked her little finger at me, demonstrating its independence. 'Like waving to a friend: *bye bye.*' I imitated her movement and waved back to her, but at the piano I still used my little finger as an approximate edge to my hand. It took me a decade to understand its possibilities: the tiny candle-lights it sets at the top of a melody, its sleigh-bells, its *coloratura*, its left-hand foundations and invitations.

We began work on Bach's small preludes.

'Bach basically is father of all music,' she told me. 'He has *huge* influence on everybody. He was educator of Chopin, of Beethoven, of Schumann. And even all modern jazz already here. You can try anything, and Bach already do it. Of course, Bach never knew piano.'

'Why not?'

'Piano not yet invented.'

I glanced dubiously at my father, who gave an emphatic nod.

'But piano absolutely instrument of imagination, and we can create anything on it. Clear organ here.' She demonstrated a small prelude. 'Remember always that Bach represents God in this world, with his wisdom, his acceptance, his forgiveness. Like he always bless you.'

'I've already learnt that prelude,' I told her, imagining it was possible to complete a piece. 'I finished it with my old teacher.'

'Bach is never finished. Life in this music *endless*.' She took my finger and dived with it into the key; it plunged to the bottom with the precise weight of a ball bearing. 'And here, *very* harpsichord touch. What Bach gives? Peace, of course, and bells.'

The evenness she demanded went well beyond the physical handicaps of a lazy fourth finger or attention-seeking thumb. It was an evenness of thought, a spiritual discipline. 'We play with our ears,' she reminded me. 'Seeing ears, hearing eyes. Clever heart, warm brain.'

My hands, brown with the Australian sun, tripped across the keyboard beside hers, as pink and round as starfish. 'Not,' she said, as I guessed at a sound, and then she took my hand and guided my fingers to the right attack. Often I didn't even register the precise spins she put on every sound; I was as tone-deaf to inflexion as a person speaking a foreign tongue. To me the keys of the piano were still on–off buttons, which could be played loud, or soft, or somewhere in between.

❋

At home, I was not yet practising two hours a day, but I told my friends that I was. On one camping trip with our neighbours, around the fire, I gave a self-aggrandising account of my life as a junior concert pianist. As we drove home the following day, my brother and baby sister dozed beside me.

I closed my eyes and pretended to be asleep too, so that I could listen to my parents speaking *sotto voce* in the front.

'Lizzie thinks we're pushing Anna,' said my mother. 'That she's missing out on a childhood.'

'That's bullshit,' said my father. 'Did you tell her how much she enjoyed the piano?'

'I told her about the little stories she makes up for her pieces. But Lizzie said that this only proved her point. That this was her way of getting the childhood she was missing out on. She said it was one of the most tragic things she had ever heard.'

I lay in the backseat and rehearsed this in my mind. *Tragic. Me. Missing out on a childhood.* The melodrama of it delighted me; a tear of the most exquisite self-pity formed in my eye and then rushed down my cheek. I let it dry on my skin. If I wiped it away, they would know I had been eavesdropping.

In fact my parents rarely pushed me to practise. 'Practice makes perfect,' my mother said occasionally. I was not sure that I believed her, but I took it on faith, like so much in childhood. Sometimes my father sat beside me when I practised; sometimes he sat behind me in the study and wrote poetry.

Usually, I was glad to play the piano. I was an uncoordinated child, and playing an instrument offered me purchase on the physical world: a small realm of possible mastery. Each night, my parents took me out the back for remedial ball skills.

'Hands ready,' my mother coached, as my father lobbed a soccer ball at me. It approached with the precision of a heat-seeking missile, its black and white hexagons swirling towards my face.

'Catch!' they cried out, in unison.

I always lost my nerve at the key moment.

'You'll never catch it if you don't *look at it*,' my mother re-peated, running inside to fetch a flannel. I waited for my nose to stop bleeding, and then returned to the piano.

Every now and then I resented it, and Lizzie's words echoed in my head. One Saturday morning, I rallied the neighbourhood children in a new business venture. We sifted the neighbours' driveway, searching for pieces of gravel of the utmost beauty and rarity, which we painted in watercolours – sapphire, amethyst, ruby and emerald – and marketed to passers-by as 'precious stones'. We had sold four bundles before lunch-time, including one to a stranger, clearing twelve cents in profit, when I had to return home to practise Bach. My father sat behind me in the study, typing a short story; behind him, three windows framed a Saturday sky. It was a sky that was blue with possibility: a sky that contained my missing childhood.

I slammed the piano lid shut: 'I hate Bach.' The words felt blasphemous in my mouth: I knew immediately that this was a much greater sin than hating Stevie Wonder.

At my piano lesson the following Tuesday, my father gave me a mischievous look and turned to Mrs Sivan. 'Anna said she hated Bach.'

'No, I didn't!'

Mrs Sivan remained very calm. 'Of course you did not. It is impossible. Bach chooses himself who he will like, and who he will not.'

❋

At the end of the year, there was to be a concert in Elder Hall at the University of Adelaide.

'We have excellent name,' Mrs Sivan said. She collected English words like small coins, and her cache was overtaking mine. '*A Spectrum of Piano Music.*'

'That *is* an excellent name,' said my father.

'You like, yes?' She flushed with pleasure and turned to me. 'The stage must be like another room in your house. When you step out there, you smile at your friends, you bow, you enjoy sharing your music. You feel like fish.'

'A fish in water?'

'Of course.'

At nine, I fancied myself a veteran of the stage because of my starring role as Fairy Queen in the Year 3 operetta. My mother had made my first diva frock, with a satin, sequinned bodice and tulle skirt. Armed with a cardboard wand coated in glitter, I had stepped out onto the stage and found myself at home. On the final night, as I delivered a bouquet of flowers to Mrs Vaughan at the piano, a smile seized control of my face and threatened to consume my head.

A Spectrum of Piano Music promised an equal glory. It was to be on 18 September; all other dates in the calendar now existed in relation to this one. In our lessons, we moved through the small preludes and the *Anna Magdalena Notebook* to the inventions and sinfonias. Mrs Sivan took me through each part repeatedly, considering the intention of each note, the attraction that bound it to its neighbours. It was not enough to play each part, to feel it in my hands: I had to sing it in my head, follow its contour, tell its story. Then, when I put the parts together, by a sudden miracle I could hear them all at once. It was as though I had three minds, or three sets of ears, operating in parallel. The first time this happened, I turned to her, astonished. My consciousness had expanded; I could feel air rushing into unused parts of my mind. 'Exactly!' she said. 'Otherwise will be *awful*.'

As the concert drew nearer, my lessons became longer. After one lesson in the school holidays, I went to my best friend Sophia's house for a sleepover.

'What took you so long?' she asked. 'We've been waiting to watch *Thriller*!'

'My first two-hour lesson,' I explained smugly.

In our lessons, Mrs Sivan sat beside me at the piano, seizing my hand and correcting it, forming my fingers into shape, or playing alongside me two octaves above, the intensity of her sounds ringing in my ears: 'Do you know how little is different? But huge, *huge*. This we call science in arts. The more you understand each little thing, the more you understand all.'

As I played, she talked or sang with the music. Sometimes, she asked me to move aside and played for me, but this was rare. 'I don't want you to *copy*, monkey-style.'

She explained the circle of fifths to me, piling fifths one above the other, always brightening, until we arrived back in the key where we had begun. I blinked, amazed: it was improbable as an Escher drawing. Then she unravelled us through perfect fourths, travelling backwards past G-flat major and C-flat major, with their great hoards of flats, returning to the daylight of C major. The mathematics of it delighted me.

'Do you understand?' she asked.

'Yes,' I replied.

She turned to my father, beaming. 'I have never met such an intelligent nine-year-old, who can understand at first telling the circle of fifths.'

At such moments, I walked out of her lessons sky-high, unassailable. At other moments, I felt smaller. When I was tiring, she would stop and address me urgently.

'What is we need is to feed our spirit, constantly. And feeding ourselves with other people's food is not great nutrition for our soul. Must digest. Look sometimes at people growing older, and wisdom coming inside. Start of what I call *digested wisdom.*'

In the early days, these speeches baffled me, and I sat there with eyes averted, trying to make myself as inconsequential as possible. When the great force of her conversation halted at a question mark, I ventured a tentative yes or no, searching her face for the right answer.

'You are too intelligent a girl to guess,' she reprimanded me once. 'What comes after translation? *Interpretation.* First you must translate composer's wishes exactly, and then you're free to do interpretation, otherwise you *automatically* restricted.'

As she offered me this, I snuck a glance at the clock. Soon I would be back in the car with my father, tracing those dark streets back home to Nailsworth, where my mother would be preparing dinner. Then I could settle in to watching *Diff'rent Strokes*, and it would be another six days before my next lesson.

※

The dress rehearsal for *A Spectrum of Piano Music* was held on a sunny spring afternoon, but there was a hushed twilight in the imposing hall, with its dark wood and red plush seats. Mrs Sivan's high-school students were scattered around the auditorium, exuding adolescent cool. I walked in holding my mother's hand, and immediately regretted my lolly-pink overalls.

When it was my turn to play, I climbed up on the stage, grimaced at my mother's enthusiastic applause and began a Bach sinfonia. I had rehearsed the opening many times with Mrs Sivan, until the small bells of its *moto perpetuo* had become second nature and my hearing automatically expanded to accommodate its three voices. But as I progressed to the second line, a worry intruded: *What does the left hand do next? Imagine if I had a memory lapse in front of all these high-school students!* The individual parts lost their focus, and the three dimensions of sound contracted back into one.

'Not hearing!' Mrs Sivan announced from the audience.

I stopped and started again.

'Not!' She called out an instruction which I couldn't hear, so I kept playing.

'Never just playing but hearing *inside!*' she exclaimed, but my grandparents had said my sinfonia was excellent when I played it at Sunday lunch, so I continued.

'We will work!' she called out, and climbed up from the audience onto the stage. As she started talking to me again about depths, or about not sitting, or about breathing spaces, or about all the other things I was not doing, I felt overwhelmed and started to cry.

'My darling, what is this?' She wrapped her arm around me. 'Always can be better, always growing. You must not cry, except for good tears, when you are so moved by the music.'

Against my will, my bad tears continued. I was so humiliated to be crying in front of high-school students that I started heaving with sobs. My mother stepped up to the stage.

'I think I might take her outside for some fresh air.'

'Of course,' said Mrs Sivan. 'Enjoy beautiful day, and then we continue.'

My mother took my hand and walked me down the aisle, past the staring high-school students, into the spring day outside.

'I don't understand,' I wailed, my shameful secret now public.

She held me to her and rocked me in her arms. 'Don't be a goofy goat,' she said, as the afternoon sun beat down on us, and my pink overalls dug into my crotch, and the oblivious adult world continued around us.

When we returned to the hall, Mrs Sivan put her arm around me and led me back to the stage and pulled up a chair so that we could work.

'My darling, life in music always learning, always growing. What is the difference between good and great musician?'

I knew the answer by now, even if I did not yet understand it.

'Little bits,' I said.

'Exactly!' she replied, delighted. 'Little bit more hearing, little bit more freedom.'

She had to tell me everything. She had to fit out this alternative universe for me, item by item, word by word, sound by sound. It is never enough to tell a student something once: teaching is constant repetition, constant correction. She repeated her lessons and anecdotes as a musician performs repertoire: each time reinterpreted, and so made new.

On the stage of Elder Hall she again took me through the breathing spaces and conducting lines of this sinfonia. I played with a heavy-handed punctuation, inking every musical sentence with an emphatic full-stop. 'Do not sit,' she reminded me. 'Bach never stops.' In Bach, every ending is also a beginning. Over time I came to understand the quiet that lies at the heart of his *moto perpetuo*.

She held a lot back in those early years, but gave the maximum I could take, and a little more. Gradually, I came to know more of her ideas by heart. By the time I properly understood them, they were absorbed into my body, and I could no longer tell where her ideas began and mine left off.

'This is good,' she said to me later, 'this means this knowledge has come to you. It is *intuition*.' She grinned at this sparkling new word. 'In-tuition. It means tuition that has come *inside*.'

On Friday night at the concert, there were three chairs lined up in the green room. One of Mrs Sivan's adult students, Debra Andreacchio, supervised the performers backstage, ushering us from one chair to the next, each time closer to the stage. Sitting in the third chair, I imagined what it would feel like to be sitting in the first chair, and then I was in it, and now I was onstage, trying to remember to smile at my friends and bow and enjoy sharing my music – and then it was over. It was easier than the rehearsal, and nobody had stopped me. Through the transformative ritual of a performance, Elder Hall had become somewhere warm, somewhere victorious.

At interval, Mrs Sivan gave me a fragrant embrace, and I joined my parents and grandparents in the audience for the second half. As the last performer left the stage, my grandfather leant forward in his chair.

'It would appear that nobody has prepared a speech,' he observed, and strode purposefully down to the front.

'Good evening, ladies and gentlemen. On one of my inspections of the Woodville High Special Music Centre, I was fortunate to hear Mrs Sivan's remarkable teaching, and I drew the conclusion immediately that she was an out-of-the-ordinary teacher of the piano. I feel that after tonight's wonderful treat these initial impressions have been truly vindicated.'

My father winked at my mother; my own triumph burnt quietly inside me. The rhythm of my adult life had begun.

Chapter 2. Mozart

THE FOLLOWING MONTH, I sat my Third Grade piano examination at Mrs Sivan's house. The examiner was a teacher from the conservatorium, Miss Stokes. 'Very good examiner, really,' Mrs Sivan told me. 'Serious, respectful and respectable.'

Miss Stokes was tall and grave and distinguished, and sat behind a bridge table with the upright posture of a ballerina. As I played my program, I was aware of a second invisible audience behind the kitchen door: Mrs Sivan, silently conducting me from the kitchen table; Debra, who had prepared my general knowledge and aural tests; and my father, anxiously pinching his neck.

'There are certainly a lot of pieces in your Extra List,' Miss Stokes observed, after I had played the required program. 'Can you really play them all?'

'If you want me to.' I launched into a Mozart sonata, the first of my nine extra pieces.

'Thank you, dear,' she said, when I came to the end of the first movement. 'That will be all.'

Later that week, shortly before dinner, my father answered the phone in the kitchen. He whooped and gave the thumbs up: 'A-plus!'

I felt stunned. My parents had warned me that nobody ever received an A-plus, that an A-plus was the stuff of legend, and here I was, struck by one. He handed me the phone.

'This examiner very excited,' Mrs Sivan was saying. 'Really, she *never* gives A-plus! *Splendid technical development.* What is this word, *splendid*?'

'It means very good.'

I returned the phone to my father and stared around the kitchen, relocating myself in normality. The pasta bubbled on the stove where he had abandoned it; the kitchen's black and white tiles stretched away on either side of us, seemingly to infinity. Mrs Sivan's happy, frantic voice to my father was insect-small, but still contained all her presence, all her weight, and then my mother's car zipped up the driveway and I ran to the door to tell her, so I could experience my A-plus all over again.

'Very good news, really,' Mrs Sivan said at our next lesson. 'The examiner was so happy and excited by your playing. Told she had never heard sonata form so good, so strong, so logically connected. She wants you go to conservatorium and play your program for all other examiners.'

The conservatorium! The word seemed to contain the heft of that imposing building.

My father sat up. 'Terrific!'

'Of course! You enjoy this music, and immediately you want to share! Real music always coming *from*, and going *to*, and moving power of the music always love. And is good for these people to know your name. Like – how do you say?' She scanned the room, settling on a box of tissues. 'Like Kleenex.'

My father laughed. 'Like a brand-name.'

'Exactly.'

'And all experience good for *practising concert.* Psychology of stage very precise and very important. In all your inquisitive mind, in all your *merciless demanding* of yourself in every little detail, you must be confident onstage. Happy! Not like person who walks around with nose in air, knows everything in between concerts. *Snob.*' She said the word with special relish, placing her finger on her nose and directing it upwards. 'But then onstage opposite. Like *baby.* Helpless. Always do more than you say. This is real power.'

She took a small white booklet from the top of her piano and presented it to my father. I craned to read its title: *The Adelaide Eisteddfod Society: Syllabus with Entry Form and Rules.* My heart quickened. I had outgrown my ambitions for *Young Talent Time*, but some archetype remained.

'Do you think Anna is ready to enter this?' my father asked.

'Only if going in with right intention. We don't go in competitions for to win: music is not a sport. The aim is *opposite.* Chance to share your music. Give a lot of your visions, bring your excitement about it. We go in competitions *by the way.* Really, I hate competitions in big sense, but if you can use them for yourself, then okay. Can be useful training for concerts.'

My father leafed through the syllabus with growing excitement. 'She could enter this one – *Ten years and under, own choice* – and here's another – *Australian composition.* And given what you said about the sonata, surely she should also go for this Mozart prize?'

'Of course. But we must go deeper and do more mature, because expectation comes already. Please, take Mozart and we will work.'

I reached into my music bag and took out the Mozart sonata, though I didn't really understand why we had to work more on it, since it had already been certified with an A-plus.

'Who is Mozart?' she asked.

'A very good composer,' I offered.

'Absolute genius composer, of course. But more: he was music himself. And we have only one Mozart. In my opinion was face of the God. Of course, this made it hard for people to accept. If you find the sort of person very hard-working is fine, you can immediately explain, make easy. But this was *beyond*. What people didn't understand; was not easy – was *complete*. All job was done before, only results now.'

Perhaps I was now in a similar position: after the job of the past year, I could now sit back and enjoy the completed results. But as I began the first bar, she stopped me.

'Not. Pedal completely wrong. What Mozart created? This *oily legato*. His touch itself is pedal. You can still use pedal – yes – but not like a connection, only like conducting support. And remember, always vocal hearing.' She demonstrated the movement's opening at the top of the piano. Even in this tinkling register, the sound was that of a *coloratura* soprano, of improbable, superhuman range. 'This music so positive! So giving! Remember, Mozart was born with happy of everything. First of all, he was happy child, because his music gave him everything. And his father was near him with a lot of love and support and giving. People say his father was a despot, awful, but is really enormous luck to have such supportive father.'

My father transcribed this diligently into his notebook.

'I myself have some understanding – for me piano was everything – so how Mozart was robbed I don't really understand. Mozart was a little spoilt, yes. But he was spoilt by God. What looks to him natural, other people have to work, one lifetime not enough. And at same time, Mozart always kept this quality of a child. Wise child.'

We began the sonata again, and as she demanded more hearing, more vocal touch, more simplicity, this known sonata became again unknown and perfection receded from my grasp.

'Is endless job, *endless*,' she agreed, as we were leaving. 'With second-rate composer we can reach, sometimes, but with Mozart we always going deeper and deeper and deeper and never reach. Is full lifetime job, unlimited, but *incredibly* rewarding.'

※

Several months later, on a cold Sunday afternoon, I arrived at the Maylands church hall, venue of the Adelaide Eisteddfod, dressed in my best red skirt and matching jumper. I pretended I was there by the way, but I was really there to claim my future. My mother took me out the back, where a stern volunteer assigned me a number.

'Number 14, can you remember that?' my mother asked.

'Of course.'

'Good luck, darling!' She planted a kiss on my cheek, and left to join my father and grandparents in the audience. I handed over my music to the volunteer, the last of my earthly goods, and ventured backstage. It was under-lit and cold there, with damp, moss-green carpet. I sat down beside a small radiator and tried to warm my hands, which felt as brittle as glass.

A small blonde girl approached me.

'What grade are you doing?' she asked, by way of introduction.

'Grade Four,' I replied, with quiet modesty. The previous month I had played at the conservatorium for the examiners' convention, with two older girls. They had also completed their Grade Three exams that year, but had received a B and a C. *A commendable effort*, I had told them, with a renewed sense of my own distinction.

'What about you?'

'Grade Five.'

I looked at her sceptically. 'What mark did you get for Grade Four?'

'A-plus,' she said, as a Chinese girl vogued into the room, wearing a pink fur coat.

'That's Evelyn Chua,' the blonde girl whispered. 'She's doing Grade Eight.'

'No way!' It had not occurred to me that children were capable of such things.

'She's a child prodigy.'

Evelyn caught my eye and looked away, and said something to her mother and laughed. When the adjudicator's bell rang, she removed her coat, revealing a tiny white pinafore, and hastened to the stage.

'Number 14!' a volunteer called out. 'I'd like you to come up now, too.'

I farewelled my new friend and followed the volunteer up to the wings, where I could see Evelyn perform. She played Copland's *The Cat and the Mouse*, which is a humorous piece, almost a cartoon soundtrack, but which I experienced as a type of violence, as it catapulted me from my innocent self-belief. Evelyn performed it as if she were dancing at the piano, with extravagant arm movements underlining its technical difficulty. She might not have captured its wit, but she terrified the ten-year-old standing behind her in the wings.

'Well done,' I said breathlessly, as she came off the stage to thunderous applause.

'Are you *kidding*? That was terrible. That was the *worst ever.*'

I crept out onto the stage in a state of shock and delivered an apologetic Bach sinfonia. Throughout my performance, Evelyn's *Cat and Mouse* ran through my mind in unflattering counterpoint. Afterwards I forgot to bow and ran from the stage to join my parents in the audience.

'Well done, Pie,' my father said, miserably.

'I didn't like the piece that Evelyn Chua played at all,' said my mother.

Contestant 18 was next: Sebastian Lee. He wore a private-school uniform even though it was Sunday, with the blue striped shirt rakishly untucked. After a neat, quick bow, he sat at the piano and contemplated the keys for a moment, before winding the seat up several rotations, and then several more. He examined the ceiling, took a handkerchief out of his pocket, and wiped his brow. Then he flexed his fingers and launched suddenly into Debussy's 'Golliwogg's Cakewalk' from *Children's Corner*.

'Goodness gracious, wasn't that something!' my grand-mother marvelled, almost falling out of her chair.

Perhaps these were the children Lizzie should have been concerned about: the children who sacrificed their childhoods to practice. But as I listened to them play, having a childhood no longer seemed all it was cracked up to be. *How these children were robbed I did not understand.*

Afterwards the adjudicator stepped up to the front and tweaked his bow-tie. 'I would like to congratulate all the children who performed this afternoon.'

My mother drummed her fingers against her knee; my pulse beat in my ears. I knew I was out of my league, but still hoped he might have recognised something in my playing that I hadn't been aware of myself.

'Let us bear in mind that all the children who performed today were winners of a sort.'

The audience leant into him with its great bruising need.

'First prize goes to competitor number 9,' he announced, and Evelyn sprang up to collect her prize.

'Why does her mother dress her like a baby?' my mother asked, too loudly.

'Second prize goes to a very fine performance by competitor number 18,' he continued.

Sebastian shrugged and went to the front to collect his report.

'And I would like to award an honourable mention to a modest but charming performance by competitor number 14.'

'Hell's bells!' my mother sang out. 'That's you, Pie!'

I walked out to the front and shook the adjudicator's hand.

'Congratulations,' he said, looking over my head.

Afterwards, I lined up behind Sebastian to collect my report. 'I came second in this section when I was four years old,' he told me, with a handsome grin. I blushed, flattered that such a celebrity in my universe should speak to me, and grabbed my report and ran out to the car.

A nicely controlled performance, and final chords good.

I pored over these words, searching their nooks and crannies for some sort of proof, and then passed the report to my parents in the front seat so that they could do the same.

'Of course I could make you child prodigy,' Mrs Sivan said at my next lesson.

My heart quickened. *Could you, please?*

'But I am not interested in instant results. More important is your future. About music coming inside. Never rely on competitions. Never build your life on it. Competitions must be used *for* yourself. Altogether, I never feel envy. Opposite! If someone else can do it, I'm happy! Is great for music! And always remember: if someone else can do it, *so can I.*'

If Evelyn Chua could be a child prodigy, then so could I, and if Mrs Sivan was not going to make me into one, I would secretly do it myself. When we returned to the first movement of the Mozart sonata, I incorporated undulating arm movements, as I had seen Evelyn do.

'What is this?' She looked astounded. 'Butterfly technique? Of course, I never say *never.* We can go from Adelaide to Melbourne through *Perth.* Is possible. But what for? Life is too short! Always better to take direct route, to be economical, to *save your energy.* Exactly like walking. I think much better to put one foot in front of the other, yes? Not like this.'

She stood up to demonstrate, zigzagging across the room. 'Compliment is not *it sounds difficult*. For true artist everything looks easy! All looks natural! When I see Baryshnikov, Nureyev, I too think I can dance.'

She sat back down beside me. 'Playing the piano is choreography. Possibilities *endless*. We clap, we embrace, we dance, we sprinkle – what is it? – icing sugar! But these are motivated movements coming from need, coming from intention. We fly with our sounds, not with our arms,' she said, and flapped her arms for me, a caricature of the playing I sought to emulate.

If I was not allowed to mimic these children's techniques, I could at least apply some of their polish. They had a surface gloss on them: they played loudly and softly in the right places, and delivered their performances in neat packages. I had seen their scores backstage, marked up in coloured pencil by their teachers: red for loud, green for soft. But Mrs Sivan was not interested in dynamics for their own sake. 'You must find emotional responses to your dynamics. *Pianissimo* can mean lullaby, or it can mean enormous tragedy, you have lost your voice.' She chuckled. 'And of course, *pianissimo* for elephant is still *fortissimo* for rabbit.'

I ignored her words and concentrated instead on decorating my music, on making a phrase swoon.

'Not! Never demonstrate,' she reprimanded me. 'Never beautify Mozart. He is beautiful enough already. He does not need your *make-up*. Which composer has perfect taste?'

'Mozart,' I ventured.

'Of course. Mozart and Chopin. Not one note can be changed. Not *one!* Sometimes Chopin makes revisions. But this different. This is insecurity. His first choice is always right. But Mozart!'

Her irritation evaporated and her face took on the radiance of a child.

'Mozart's simplicity is exact opposite of primitivism. Has come through full circle, after complexity.' She sketched a circle for me on my notebook, with primitivism on one side, moving through complexity, to simplicity. 'And Mozart always opera! Always vocal hearing. So theatrical and so playful. Mozart exactly like Midas: every sound he touches turns into song.'

She grasped my hand and massaged the fleshy pad just beneath my fingertip. 'Here, with pad of finger. Vocal touch. Still this evenness, of course – comes from root of harpsichord.' She demonstrated a scale in Bach's style, a crystal-clear succession of bells. 'But injected with voice, joined together in pearly legato,' and she threaded the same scale through with song.

It took me some time to understand her pearly legato. Then one day, as she played me Mozart, I could suddenly see the faces on each of her sounds, hear their individual appeals to the listener, and I started to cry.

'What is it?' she asked.

'There is a smile in each of your sounds.'

She beamed, and embraced me. 'My darling, this is how I know that you are mine.'

The following week, I brought my Mozart sonata to the Adelaide Eisteddfod, with its fragile cargo of pearly legato, of song. Sebastian played first, and as I listened to him from the wings, Evelyn snuck up the stairs and waved her arms in the air beside me.

'What are you doing?' I asked.

She gave me a daredevil grin. 'Trying to put him off.'

I felt a righteous indignation. 'Music is love,' Mrs Sivan had told me, 'love is the moving power of music.' Watching Evelyn's frantic waving, I recognised the rift between Mrs Sivan's teaching, and the imperfect world in which I would try to enact it. These children approached music shamelessly as sport; I tried for contempt, but also felt some envy. After Sebastian had finished, he chased Evelyn down the stairs, laughing, and I felt disappointed that she did not bother to stay in the wings to put me off, too.

I stepped onto the stage, and marched over to the piano, but when I sat down, I realised I had lost middle C. The world's compass point had disappeared. I moved my hands up and down above the keyboard, hovering above one C and then another, hoping my body would remember it for me.

It was a Sunday; half of my family was there. From the stage I could hear groans, small noises of despair.

'*She's forgotten it!*' my great-grandmother called out, triumphantly.

I stared at the keyboard; it stared back at me. Stalemate. I didn't see any way out of this, so I launched into a chipmunk's rendition of the opening phrase, an octave too high. The shock almost threw me off my stool, but I dropped an octave and concluded the piece at pitch, crippled with shame.

This time, when Evelyn received first prize, I received nothing, not even an honourable mention. *It's great for music*, I told myself.

I brought Mrs Sivan the report, as if it might teach her something. She scanned through its collection of stock phrases.

After a bit of an unhappy start, you certainly threw yourself into it. An admirable clarity in this performance, but pedal was over-used.

'How possible to have admirable clarity at same time as pedal over-used?' she asked. 'Complete contradiction! Do they take these comments out of – how do you say – little book?'

'Phrasebook,' said my father.

'Yes exactly, phrasebook. The big mistake is making art into sport. Impossible. Of course you must respect opinion, because otherwise will become cynical, and lose sounds automatically. But *never ever* rely on them. If you try to please everybody, you automatically will be robot, or lost in jungle.'

Chapter 3. Shostakovich

SHORTLY AFTER SHE ARRIVED in Adelaide, Mrs Sivan had been invited to the Elder Conservatorium by its director, Clemens Leske, to present a recital and masterclass. Now she was appointed to its teaching staff, and suggested I audition for its specialist training program. It was only six months since I had been to the conservatorium for the examiners' convention, but now, as I wandered down its long corridors with my mother, something had changed; the air felt heavier.

We arrived at the piano room, and I peered through the small porthole in its airlocked double doors. A panel of three examiners talked seriously to each other at a desk, silent as mime artists, while a glossy Steinway stood open before them. I recognised Miss Stokes, but neither of the men. As I watched, a white-haired man nodded gravely and wrote something on a piece of paper.

'Sit down, darling one,' my mother said. 'Relax.'

I sat down on the vinyl chair in the hallway and took out my music. In my lessons, we had been working on Shostakovich's

Dances of the Dolls, small pieces that Mrs Sivan had played for the composer as a child.

'Shostakovich was epitome of dignity, of culture, of moral,' she had said. 'Just unbelievable quality this man was. Was *impossible* to sit when he's coming in a room. Was beyond us, beyond everybody – believe me, I watch it. And of course highest level of pianistic culture. Remember, piano's choreography is beyond human imagination. No one ballet dancer can use so many varieties of choreography. Here we are *dropping position*. But here clapping!' She had laughed as she played, her hands springing to life like two small puppets.

Now my mother drummed her fingers against the back of my chair, as I tried to summon this dance into my mind.

'Can you please stop doing that?' I muttered.

'Doing what?' She wrapped her arms tight around her torso, clinging to her blouse.

The double doors creaked, and Miss Stokes emerged. She gave me a faint smile. 'We're ready for you now.'

I looked at my mother. Her blouse was crumpled all the way down her sides. 'Good luck, Pie,' she said, as Miss Stokes closed one door on her, and then the other.

Inside, I presented the panel with my scores. 'What would you like to play first?' a grey-haired man asked, peering at me over his glasses.

'Shostakovich, please,' I replied, and sat down at the large piano. I tried to ignore the thumping in my chest. *Never start until you are ready. Learn to listen to silence, atmospheric silence.* I gazed at the light spilling through the outside window, at the birds startling the trees. University students walked past wearing backpacks, oblivious to the room's large drama.

The white-haired man cleared his throat. 'When you're ready.'

I launched into the 'Lyrical Waltz', and at once Mrs Sivan was there beside me. *Opening four bars are clear invitation to dance. This C in left hand wants to go to F, yes? To visit his friend. And now comes beautiful melody, queen absolutely, and here this G sharp must be fully alert!* In my lesson, she had widened her eyes to show me this alertness; now, as I played, I could see her watchfulness in the G sharp. *Dancing coming around more and more, greater and greater excitement, until dolls come to life, and all is dancing!* The heaviness of the room receded, until I was this doll, dancing through air. *What this is music! Music itself excitement of the life in your hands, just like you live and breathe!* I came to the final line, and a perfect cadence deposited me back into the conservatorium, where there was silence except for the industrious scratching of pens.

'Thank you,' Miss Stokes said, thinly.

What happened now? Was I allowed to leave? I glanced at the door's porthole and caught the anxious glint of my mother's spectacles.

'What would you like to hear next, Mr Dosser?' Miss Stokes asked.

'Perhaps some Mozart,' the white-haired man suggested, and beamed at me. It was easier to play, warmed by that smile.

'Thank you, dear,' Miss Stokes said, when I came to the end of the first movement. 'That will be all.'

It was some time before I received the results. As the days went by, my waiting became more desperate, and I searched for clues everywhere.

If the next car that drives down our street is a blue car, I will get into the conservatorium.

If the next car is a red car, I will not get in, and my little sister will contract rabies.

There were portents everywhere, I realised, if you knew where to look. I dared not tell anyone: if my parents found out, they would surely lock me away. And so I furtively counted the number of Cheezels in each packet I bought from the school tuckshop, pondering whether a broken Cheezel should be rounded up to one or down to zero, and whether a prime number of Cheezels augured well, as opposed to a multiple of three.

'To be pianist is great detective job,' Mrs Sivan reminded me, as I extended this detective job to my life, searching everywhere for clues. 'You must have eyes that hear, ears that see. You must miss not one detail! *Not one!* In Shostakovich, every sign is important.'

In my scores, she circled the details I missed with her authoritative 2B pencil: articulation, dynamic markings, pedalling. She also pencilled in the punctuation, with extravagant vertical lines. Like most children, I was reluctant to breathe in my playing, to observe a comma, a *luftpause*, as if a moment's space would cause an audience to turn on its heel and leave. Gradually she guided me to an understanding of musical grammar. But grammar alone was not enough.

'Not!' she would say, seizing my hand. 'You are informing. I am not interested in *information in music*. You must listen.'

'Not!' she said, when I corrected myself. 'You are demonstrating. You are showing us what a good girl you are. You are … what is this?' She pulled another word from her hat: *'Pedantic!'*

My father nodded and transcribed this into his notebook: *Do not be pedantic.*

'The subjective is built up on objective visions,' she continued. 'To be great artist, of course you must first be great scientist, you must understand every little thing! Without organisation, it is chaos. Anarchy. But without freedom, it is … dead. It is *post-mortem examination*.'

My father laughed, and I glared at him.

'I repeat: music is logically organised fantasy. You must develop your emotional logic. And your taste. People say we can't discuss taste. Of course.' She grinned, widely. 'We can't discuss taste, on one condition: if you have it.'

In my practice at home, I tried to develop my taste, but it was difficult. I was not allowed to 'beautify' my music, like the children at the eisteddfods, but nor was I allowed to 'inform' with it. It left little room for manoeuvre.

'Of course there are many ways of being wrong,' Mrs Sivan told me. 'But to get to right destination we have not so many choices.' As I worried about my audition results, this right destination receded further. I worked on a chord progression in Shostakovich's polka, and imagined failing my audition, so that this thought adhered to the harmony, and every time I cycled back to that place, I felt a renewed disappointment. There was a passage in the gavotte that I had to play seven times perfectly, with my eyes shut. Otherwise I would fail the audition, my parents would divorce, and my sister would turn out to be a late-diagnosed dwarf.

At last the letter arrived, with the Elder Conservatorium insignia on the front. I was accepted: my sister would continue to grow; the demons vanished back into the Cheezels packet.

I called Mrs Sivan to tell her.

'Really, I am not surprised. With your levels and maturity it would be impossible not to accept.'

She rarely complimented me on my playing, and I took this response as the highest praise.

At Sunday lunch, my grandfather made a toast: 'I would like to congratulate Anna, whose dedication and hard work has already paid off handsomely. As she well knows, her grandmother and I are also keen pianists. Her grandmother excels particularly at sight-reading.'

'I'd hardly say *excel*,' my grandmother said, as she stood to clear the table.

'My wife has very few faults, of which an over-developed modesty is one. I maintain my high regard for her sight-reading. I would even be so bold to suggest that music runs down this side of the family.'

'And the other side as well,' my mother interrupted. 'Both of my grandmothers were pianists, and my sister was accepted into the conservatorium.'

'Is that right? What a marvellous achievement! In that case, I will have to revise my statement, and suggest that music runs down both sides of the family.' He chortled. 'Perhaps we should take a few moments now to consider the history of the conservatorium in South Australia. John Bishop, of course, was a significant figure in the development of ...'

The celebrations soon ended, and the triumph became part of the texture of my life. My acceptance made very little

difference, except that I occasionally performed at the conservatorium's lunch-hour concerts and, as an insider, now
referred to the place as 'the Con'.

Mrs Sivan continued teaching me from home, and my
father still drove me there every Tuesday afternoon. Although
my lessons officially lasted for forty-five minutes, she always
extended them to at least two hours, and there was no telling
when they would end.

❋

Gradually my technique was becoming freer, and it was easier
for me to find the sounds I wanted; the difficulty lay in imagining those sounds in the first place, in hearing a piece's interior
meaning, and not just reciting it as a sequence of notes.

'You say Shostakovich cannot write melody?' she asked
my father.

'No,' he answered, startled. 'He could definitely write
melody. Just think of the film music.' He crooned the theme
to *The Gadfly*.

'Of course. Shostakovich *greatest* melodist, and all evidence here. Only one question: whose heart can sing with
boot resting on their chest for whole life? But *Dances of the
Dolls* are works of fantasy, of escape, and of course he writes
melody.' She returned to my hands. 'Your pianism has to be
completely out of your inner emotional story. Playing the
piano is projection of the imagination.'

It is a difficult thing to transmit to a student: the importance of forming ideas in your imagination first, rather than
grasping for them at the keyboard. I still relied on my fingers,
unguided, to come up with approximate solutions. At the end

of a phrase, Mrs Sivan would grab my hand: 'Relax thumb, and listen *before* – what next?' I would play the final note. 'Not. You are sitting.' She demonstrated a different sound and immediately I recognised its rightness, its inevitability. Surely this recognition implied a prior knowledge? These sounds must have existed inside me already: why could I not find them myself?

At the end of each lesson she guided me to the door, but made no move to open it.

'You must learn to hear,' she said, eyes flashing. 'Please tell me you will do this, my darling. You must start to listen.'

'Okay.'

'Of course music is incredibly complex! A *huge* variety of synthesised parts! It is arts and literature and theatre *and* your dream in fantasy *and* your logical existence of today. Millions, *millions* of things! And definitely travel and ballet and opera and everything!'

Her face was flushed and radiant; as she waved her arms emphatically, she looked as if she might become airborne.

'Why are we so passionate about this instrument? Why are we so passionate to give the people this insight of it, and this sense of belonging to it?'

'I'm not sure.' The doorknob gleamed golden in the corner of my eye.

'Because it is incredible *interesting* life! It is life of incredible involvement and freedom and communication! And it gives you incredible respect to your own life, as existence!'

I yawned.

'Poor darling, you are tired. I forget sometimes you are not adult. Never have I known such serious child.' She looked at my father and shook her head in wonder. 'But I have something for you. Something very special.'

She hurried back into the kitchen and returned with an Easter egg.

'To understand the beauty of this world, *beauty* of *incredible* heights of the life – greatest achievement of greatest spirits of human being – is incredible. Yes, or *not*?'

'Yes,' I said, as definitively as I could, holding the Easter egg tight in my hand. If I ate it before we got home, I would not have to share it with my brother.

'You do not choose piano,' she said. 'Piano chooses himself. Piano chooses *you*.'

I was not sure that I wanted to be chosen by the piano. I loved music and enjoyed playing it, and I appreciated the way it brought me attention within the family. But I was not yet certain that I wanted to be claimed by it, for life.

For Christmas that year, my parents gave me something heavy and rectangular, wrapped in brown paper. I unwrapped it and discovered a red leather-bound book with blank handcut pages and a golden word, REPERTOIRE, embossed on the front.

'Now you can keep a record of everything you study with Mrs Sivan,' my mother said, eagerly.

It was a beautiful volume, and on seeing it I felt an immediate dismay. Why did they have to be so generous?

'Thank you. It's lovely.'

I turned away so they could not see my tears; not to become a professional pianist now was impossible.

In fact, my parents had made no such decision for me.

I had one year remaining at primary school, and we were trying to choose a high school: either the special music centre at Marryatville High, a public school; or Pembroke, an eastern-suburbs private school.

'It's too early for decisions to be made about her future,' my grandfather suggested at Sunday lunch. 'Even if she does decide to become a musician, she must receive the best education possible.'

'I couldn't agree more,' my mother said, uncharacteristically. 'Best to keep your options open.'

'Pembroke's fees are astronomical,' said my father, looking hopefully at my grandfather. 'It would be a financial strain, particularly with the music lessons.'

'As you know, I have always been a champion of the public system,' my grandfather replied.

Regardless of their discussions, I had already made the decision to go to Pembroke, where my best friend, Sophia, was a student. We spent much of the holidays sunbaking by her swimming pool, reading *Dolly* magazine, while she filled in the detail of my future life: how Georgina pashed Davo on sports day; how everyone agreed that Simon was a try-hard.

'Are you going to tell people at Pembroke that you play the piano?' she asked.

I had a fleeting glimpse of myself as martyr to my art, the jeering hordes misunderstanding me. It held a certain appeal.

'They might think you're a square,' she said.

'Okay, I won't.' I turned the magazine's page to Dolly Doctor.

Dear Dolly, can you pash a cute guy if you're wearing braces?

As long as you're careful not to bite, and keep your braces in good condition and free of food scraps, kissing in braces can be a romantic experience.

I memorised these words carefully, swotting how to be a teenager.

My imagined life at Pembroke came to occupy me more and more. As I practised, I rehearsed future conversations with the 'trendies', and in Mrs Sivan's lessons, I mulled over Sophia's latest dispatches.

'People talk about *talent*,' Mrs Sivan said. 'What is this talent? Talent does not play itself. Talent is money in the bank, only. How you spend it, this is up to you.'

I nodded absently and considered the vexed issue of mascara. Sophia told me that most of the girls at Pembroke wore make-up to school, but I knew my mother would say something sarcastic if I asked to do so.

'Can I give talent or not?' Mrs Sivan demanded, suddenly.

I had refined an ambiguous movement of my head, part nod, part shake, that could be taken either way.

'Of course not! I am not God!' She looked momentarily astonished. 'I cannot give you seeds. But I can make grow what is there. I will develop what you have to *maximum*.'

She continued talking, and I returned to my preoccupations. What did Sophia mean when she said she was 'moderately popular' at Pembroke? Was I 'moderately popular' at primary school? I shuffled through the social hierarchy in my head, trying to assess my position, when Mrs Sivan jolted me out of my reverie.

'Of course, Anna will never be concert pianist!'

I turned to my father in shock. His eyebrows shot up his forehead like two inverted commas.

'Good teacher, yes, and will always love music. But not performer. Not.'

But the A-plus! The acceptance into the conservatorium! The praise of my grandparents! I thought the piano had already chosen me.

'Of course I love this girl, so intelligent. Really, I never knew such a child. But so reserved. Wants to give right reading: *correct* and *right*. Does not understand emotional freedom and artistic representation.'

I started sniffling as soon as I was in the car. It was not that I necessarily wanted to be a concert pianist; it was just that I wanted to be *able* to be one, if I chose. Nobody had ever told me, so definitely, that a path was not open to me. I had believed all the sweet nothings whispered to the young: the world is your oyster; you can be anything you want to be; follow your dreams and they will become true. Two doors had now been slammed shut, one after the other, in an airlock as impenetrable as any at the conservatorium: the door to the concert stage, and beyond that, the door to unlimited possibility.

My father and I drove home in silence. When we arrived, I ran into my bedroom and lay down on my bed. My parents talked urgently in the kitchen, and then my mother came in, smelling of sherry.

'Don't cry, my baby,' she said resonantly. 'Don't be a silly duffer. It's too early to worry about the future. You've got years to decide what you want to do.'

My four-year-old sister burst into the room, with her scrap of rug and forbidden dummy. 'Anna's crying,' she announced.

'Poor Anna's had a big disappointment,' my mother said. 'Good girl, you give her a cuddle. I'll go out and finish tea.'

My sister climbed into bed with me, sucking loudly on her dummy. She fingered her scrap of rug in one hand and twirled a piece of my hair in the other.

'Dummies are for babies,' I told her.

She stopped sucking for a moment to consider this, and then spat it out, placing it on the shelf next to my bed where I had abandoned my repertoire book. It had been sitting there for some months, while I tried to decide whether it belonged in the music cabinet or on my bookshelf. My poor, poor repertoire book. I felt a terrible nostalgia for it, for the hope we used to share, and an acute sense of waste, as its blank pages would now go forever unmarked.

Chapter 4. Debussy

IN MY HEART, I suspected Mrs Sivan was right. I was too reserved; I did want to give right reading: correct and right. Such qualities were liabilities not only for my artistic career, but for my future social standing at Pembroke. Was there a chance that I might be a square? Or worse: a dork, a dweeb or even a geek?

'A geek is basically a square,' Sophia explained to me, when I asked for a definition. We sat on her front fence after school, plucking eucalyptus leaves off the tree and mashing them up in our hands. 'A dork is a social retard and a bit un-co. And a dweeb isn't necessarily a square, but is weedy and a little gross.'

'What's the antonym of a square?' I asked.

'Firstly, only squares use the word antonym,' she said, patiently. 'But it's probably a circle.'

'What's that?'

She considered this for a moment. 'There are girls at Pembroke who shoplift for a hobby.'

'Why?' I tried to conceal my shock.

She shrugged. 'They've tried everything else. Kissing boys and smoking cigarettes. There's nothing left in life.'

She scrunched her leaf into a ball and lobbed it at the nature strip; I divided mine into equal-sized portions, ordering them into the beginning of the Fibonacci sequence.

'Does Georgina shoplift?'

'Nah,' she said, tugging on her T-shirt beneath her chest. I had reason to suspect she was wearing a bra: yet another thing to come between us. 'But she's going to lose her virginity this year to Ben Armstrong. He's a Year 10.'

We both blushed. It was the first time either of us had mentioned sex, lurking around like a stalker.

'So is Georgina your best friend?' I asked, with a feigned casualness.

'Hard to say. All my friends are in different groups. There's Harriet, and then there's Sarah Ashby and Sarah Campbell-Jones. They're all my good friends in different ways.'

I nodded, like a tolerant spouse, but the street blurred before my eyes, as I saw Sophia sailing off without me to the land of the private school, accompanied by Georgina and Harriet and multiple Sarahs. They all wore Canterbury rugby tops and white lace-up boots, and went shoplifting as a hobby. My mother said Canterbury was overpriced, and shopped for my clothes at Target. *Tar-jay boutique*, she called it, with a phoney French accent.

'You're still my best friend outside school,' Sophia reassured me, 'but it gets harder all the time. Why won't your parents just let you go to Pembroke?'

'They've put my name down, but there's no guarantee that I'll get to go.' I sighed at the injustice. My parents were doctors

– weren't they supposed to be rich? 'We're going to talk about it again after the scholarship exam.'

She shook her head. 'Don't count on getting a scholarship. It's basically impossible. My stepbrother only got a half-scholarship, and he's a *brain*.'

At home that night, we received a Pembroke enrolment package, with a list of the uniform requirements.

'My godfather!' my mother exclaimed after she opened it. 'As if a jumper and blazer and three shirts and a skirt and three dresses and shoes and sandals and socks and stockings were not enough, they expect a different uniform for each sport they make you play!'

'Only dweebs wear sandals,' I offered. 'So don't worry about that.'

'And look at this!' She threw her head back with laughter. '*Girls are required to wear white or yellow underwear only!* How do they know? Do they line everyone up in the morning to check?'

'It's basically an honour system,' I said tersely.

'Highway robbery, more like it,' said Mum. 'As if the school fees weren't enough.'

My father sucked on his lips. 'It's a shame they don't offer music scholarships for piano. Or that you didn't learn the viola.'

'There's always the scholarship exam,' I said, though I knew it was basically impossible.

❋

Now that I was never going to be a concert pianist, I approached my next lesson warily, but Mrs Sivan greeted us with her customary warmth.

'Debussy is revolutionary, complete!' she announced, as she threw open the door. I followed her to the piano, and placed my copy of *Children's Corner* on the music stand.

She dropped her voice. 'Some people are followers, only.'

'Really?' I asked, disingenuously.

'Of course. Sheeps. But Debussy *no way*! For example, of course he is interested in jazz!' She pushed me aside at the piano and improvised an exuberant ragtime. My father tapped his foot and applauded loudly when she finished.

'So free!' she laughed. 'Debussy likes not to follow rules.'

I positioned my hands above the opening statement of 'Golliwogg's Cakewalk' and took a deep breath, hoping that this freedom might be contagious.

'Not,' she said before I could begin. 'Not playing. We must think of choreography. We must think of *dancing our fantasy*.'

'What fingering should I use?'

'Anton Rubinstein once said *play by nose*,' she chuckled. 'Most important is hearing inside. Fingering is *terribly* important but hands don't play themselves. Must play with seeing ears, with hearing eyes. With cool heart and with warm brain. People don't understand your spiritual world, your mental world, your emotional involvement and your physical representation, is how many things?'

'One?' I guessed.

'Exactly! And full connection between them.' She swivelled around in her chair to address my father. 'You ask me what talent is?'

I glared at him suspiciously. When exactly did he ask her this? The previous week, during my fit of tears, he had threatened to call her and 'have a word', but I had made him promise not to.

'Some people think pitch, some people say it's rhythm, co-ordination, animal abilities. But it's nothing in comparison with intelligence. I told: this girl *very* intelligent.'

I suppressed my smile and cast my eyes down, as if I were not only intelligent, but modest too.

'We need to respect our self, and not our ego. We need to respect our life in music, our position, our future, our achievement. Our aim must *never* be thanks and prizes and *praise*.'

She fixed me with a ferocious gaze.

'For me, compliment is not praise. Not *excellent*,' she said with a dainty smile, 'or that is very *nice*.' She fluttered her eyelashes. 'How I hate that word! Not! Compliment is to sit and work.'

She swivelled back to the keyboard, and we sat and worked.

At school, I also sat and worked. There was a group of girls in my class with scholarship aspirations, and our teacher, Miss Tormey, assigned us extension work in preparation for the state-wide exam. We collected special words to garnish our essays – *fluctuate, irrevocable, heinous* – and studied the magical decimal of pi. I was enchanted by pi, and copied it to fifty decimal points, memorising it like a piece of music. It had melodic contour and a syncopated rhythm, but it did not demand emotional freedom or artistic representation. There was a perverse pleasure in being able to get it correct and right.

On the morning of the scholarship exam, my mother dropped me at Sophia's house.

'Three point one four one five nine two six five three five eight nine seven nine three two three eight four six,' I began, as we walked in together.

'Okay, that's enough,' Sophia said, when we approached the school gates. She introduced me to Harriet and Georgina and Sarah Ashby.

'Hi!' I said breezily, imitating their eastern-suburbs vowels.

'Doesn't Jessica look *so* cute in her jumpsuit?' asked Georgina.

'Just *divine*!' said Harriet.

'*Divine*,' I echoed. I could think of nothing to add, except that the cube root of 1331 was 11, or that energy could not be created nor destroyed, only changed from one form into another. It was a relief to sit the scholarship exam.

'How did you go?' Georgina asked afterwards.

'Ghastly,' said Harriet.

'Awful,' said Sophia.

'Awful,' I agreed.

We air-kissed them goodbye and wandered home along the Parade. The low autumn sun warmed our bare legs, so we removed our shoes and felt the baked footpath beneath our toes. Sophia undid her hair and let it fall in her eyes; I did the same, and imitated her sultry walk. Each time a passing driver beeped or wolf-whistled, we spun around and pulled a face.

'Seven,' Sophia said, matter-of-factly, when we arrived at her house. 'A record.'

I was overcome with the benevolence of the day, and in the mood for confession.

'Does the number seven mean anything to you?'

'Like what?'

'It's a prime number, for one thing. Do you think that's significant?'

She screwed up her nose in disbelief. 'Don't be *mental*. It just means there are seven child molesters on the road, wolf-whistling at eleven-year-olds.'

❋

'How is your Debussy?' Mrs Sivan asked the following week, as I sat down at her piano.

'Fine, thank you,' I replied.

She became impatient. 'I wait for the day when you come to me and say I can't *live* without Debussy, I am *passionate* about this music, my *existence* is in these sounds.'

Her eyes blazed, and I stared back at her, chastised. I couldn't imagine these words coming out of my mouth. I wouldn't trust them. Imagine saying something like that at Pembroke next year, to Harriet or Georgina!

'Debussy is painting alive,' she continued, more mildly. She opened my *Children's Corner* to the 'The Little Shepherd'. 'Not interested in this shepherd as character, at what he is feeling and thinking. *No way!* Debussy interested in this little shepherd only as picture.'

She played the opening flute solo, applying her hands to the keyboard like paint.

'Listen to acoustic effect,' she whispered. 'Vibration … reverberation … reflection.'

I could almost see ripples in the air, as the sound travelled to the walls and returned to us.

'You think I cannot do *crescendo* on one note?' she asked, defiantly. She drew a D from the piano and her eyes widened as, against all the laws of physics, it seemed to grow louder. 'The piano is instrument of fantasy, of projection,' she beamed. 'Limited only by your imagination.'

I felt confused. Was it possible to create a *crescendo* through sheer force of will, or was she enlisting me in a delusion? I pressed experimentally on the D. It fell to the carpet with a dull thud.

'Not, you sitting. Always listen to what sounds tell you *after*. Because sounds come back to you, and then you continue.' She played the opening for me again, catching the sound on the fly and adding another layer. 'It's like poetry inside. Always you are in communication with the continuing. That is secret of music.'

When her teaching took an abstract turn, I allowed my mind to wander. Would they have marked the scholarship exam yet? My heart palpitated. I realised I had forgotten to use the word *serendipity* in my essay.

'It's the same thing as a polite and involved conversation. Always listening, yes?'

'Yes.'

'Not only immediately respond to words, but digest. We are in *dialogue with sounds*!'

She took my fourth finger and guided it into dialogue with the sounds. 'Exactly! Already much better.' She swung back around to address my father. 'My students have lunchtime concert at the conservatorium, and of course Anna must play.'

I looked at my father, and he grinned back at me. Perhaps the piano had changed its mind and chosen me, after all.

'What should she play?' he asked.

'Debussy. And will be beautiful absolute.'

Several weeks later, my mother came into choir practice and stood grimly by the door. I felt the thrill of crisis: someone must have died. She muttered something in Mrs Slater's ear and beckoned me out to the quadrangle.

'I've just had a call from Pembroke,' she said quietly. 'You won a scholarship.'

I stared back at her.

'You received the highest mark in the state.'

'No, I didn't,' I said, suspecting a trick.

'Yes, you did, goofy goat. I've just had the principal on the phone. She's delighted by your results.'

I considered this, and decided I felt thrilled. 'Yippee!' I ventured. We clasped each other in a quick, embarrassed hug.

'It's still confidential, so you can tell Sophia, but nobody else,' she said.

That night, I called Sophia with the news.

'Bulk ex!' she said. 'Congrats. We'll be best friends again!'

Immediately it was worth it. 'Don't tell anyone else yet,' I warned her. 'It's still a secret.'

'Are you ever going to tell anyone else?'

I thought about it and decided not to. It was great that we were going to be together at Pembroke, but in some ways it would be better if my parents were paying my school fees, just like everybody else.

❈

'How is Debussy?' Mrs Sivan asked at my next lesson, as she ushered us in.

'I'm enjoying it very much,' I replied, the maximum my Anglo-Saxon reticence would allow.

'Of course. Enjoyment is incredible. I have new student, by the way. Kate. You will very like. Her emotional response is *incredible*. She is bright and happy. Even without certain foundations, she has such ... electricity.'

'How old is she?' I asked, suspiciously.

'Fourteen. So wants to know. Is enjoying *enormous*.'

'I'm also enjoying it very much,' I repeated.

'Of course. But not enough that *I enjoying very much*. Music is arts of generosity. Must also be that *I want to share my enjoyment*, my discovery, my incredible visions *with*, I want to share it with audience and I want to give it. This is what for you play concert – yes?'

'Yes,' I said, unconvinced.

'*Must* be this way, and only. I told: what you give is yours. Music is arts of love and of giving. Based on incredible respect and understanding to piece you are coming through. Otherwise is just information and playing right notes, like schoolgirl.'

But I *am* a schoolgirl, I thought. A primary schoolgirl.

'Of course, you are still schoolgirl,' she conceded. 'Doesn't matter. At concert, all other performers will be university student, except Kate. For this reason, *must* be mature.' She dropped her voice. 'I tell you one secret. When you play concert, find one person in the audience, and play for him only.' She grinned. 'Suddenly *everybody* thinks you play for him.'

And so, in the last week of term, I stepped out once more onto the stage of Elder Hall. I was dressed in my blue-checked school uniform, which felt a little out of place, but also offered protection of sorts, an appeal for mercy: *I am only a schoolgirl*. As I bowed, I scanned the audience for Sophia, who was already on school holidays. There she was in the third row, sitting between my father and her grandmother, her mouth set a little defensively. It touched me that she was here when she did not even like classical music. As I sat at the piano, I resolved to play for her. I would offer an explanation of what I did, hoping that through her, Pembroke might also understand.

It was difficult, in this large hall, to engage in dialogue with sounds; my opening flute solo dispersed outwards and upwards and vanished into the roof space. Midway through 'The Little Shepherd', I lost my bearings completely. I tried several harmonic byways, all of which were dead ends. A large silence bore down on me, magnified by four hundred listeners. I felt paralysed, but then I shrugged, with a feigned nonchalance; the correct chord winked at me and I was able to continue. My shrug was for Sophia: it said that although I might be up onstage having a memory lapse, I did not really care, because I was neither geek nor square nor dweeb.

Afterwards, I slipped out to join the audience. My father gave me an ironic smile and shifted over a seat.

'Hi!' said Sophia, casually. She had covered her program with love hearts.

'I can't believe I shrugged like that,' I whispered.

'Like what? Check out the guy two rows back! Totally Bevan from *Young Talent Time*.'

As I turned back, I caught Mrs Sivan's eye. She nodded at me, and I sank deeper in my chair. None of the students who played after me had so much as a memory lapse, let alone a shrug, and her earlier words echoed in my ears: *Of course Anna will not be concert pianist. Not.*

The final performer was Mrs Sivan's new student, Kate. She walked briskly onto the stage in a tartan taffeta skirt and launched into Liszt's Hungarian Rhapsody No. 6. The rhapsody began as a proclamation – the gypsies are coming! – and I sat up straight in my chair, forgetting about shrugs and memory lapses. In the central section, a world-weary lament, she listened to what the sounds told her after, before the distant invitation to a dance. Somewhere the dance began, and then it came closer and the stakes were raised in every repetition until everybody was dancing and even Sophia was jiggling beside me and the dance was all there was. By the time Kate reached the conclusion, she was a goddess, delivering each octave like a thunderbolt. What must it be to be up there on that stage, looking down on those hands – my hands! – doing such staggering things. This was what Mrs Sivan meant when she spoke of electricity, of emotional involvement and artistic achievement. I wanted to run back to the stage and push Kate aside and ravish that piano again, but with her teenage hands instead of my child ones.

'Heaps good,' said Sophia, as we joined in the rapturous applause. 'Who was that?'

'Kate Stevens,' I said, with a strange pride. The name resonated like a film star's.

Mrs Sivan was glowing afterwards as she hugged me. 'Of course it is impossible to – what you say – shrug onstage, and must never do it again. But you like this girl, yes?'

'Yes,' I said, resolving to pay better attention to her words. *If someone else can do it, then so can I*, she had told me. From now on, I would concentrate in my lessons, and not let her words drift by me as I thought about other things. I would start trying to *listen inside*, to share my artistic visions, to feel incredible respect and understanding.

My father delivered me back to school, but for once I could not concentrate on my work. I had a Liszt rhapsody in my ears, beckoning me into the future, and I was impatient to return home to the piano and find my way there.

PART II.

Chapter 5. Beethoven

A T MY PRIMARY-SCHOOL GRADUATION, I performed a Mozart sonata and recited a poem I had written for the occasion:

I have come to the end of a seven-year car wash
And the teachers have scrubbed me clean,
For not only have they given me an outer gloss
But a beautiful inner sheen.

Over the summer holidays, my inner sheen grew only more radiant, and I continued to work on my outer gloss. I requested a Jellyfish Swatch watch for Christmas, to match Sophia's, and spent most afternoons sunbathing by her pool.

'Are you excited about starting at Pembroke, darling?' her mother asked.

I had rehearsed an answer to this question. 'I think a more accurate word would be *anticipation*. I feel a *delightful sense of anticipation*.'

Occasionally, that sense of anticipation gave way to anxiety, but I was reassured by the thought that Sophia would be constantly by my side. We had asked to be in the same house, and had decided to study the same languages, French and Indonesian.

'Only geeks do Latin,' she had explained. 'It's a dead language, after all. And the German teacher talks through her teeth and sounds evil.'

At Sunday lunch, I informed my family of my plans to study French and Indonesian.

'I will be disappointed if you break with the family tradition of Latin scholarship,' my grandfather warned me.

'It's because she can't bear to be apart from that Sophia,' my mother told him, 'not for one moment.'

'It's not that at all,' I protested. 'It's because only geeks do Latin.'

My brother sniggered.

'I beg your pardon?' my grandfather asked.

'Latin is a dead language.'

'Ah!' he chuckled, leaning back in his chair. 'There is a flaw in your reasoning. The study of Latin is, *inter alia*, a study of roots. Such a study will remain forever current, and worthy of respect for any serious scholar, or for anyone who chooses the pursuit of knowledge over ignorance.'

I tore a small strip off my serviette and rolled it into a ball.

'Ignorance is bliss,' I said.

'Knowledge is power!' he retorted.

'Bliss is better than power.'

My father pricked up his ears. 'That's not a bad point.'

'A somewhat irresponsible position,' my grandfather

laughed. 'Fortunately, one need make no such choice. Through the study of Latin, one arrives at both bliss and power, as you will soon discover. Now that I am retired, I have time for selective projects. One of those will be to teach my grand-daughter Latin. It needn't interfere with your schoolwork, as we will concentrate our study on Saturdays.'

'I have theory lessons with Debra on Saturdays!' I protested.

'In that case, we can resort to correspondence. And of course I will be happy to discuss your homework during family lunches.'

Beneath the table I flicked my tiny serviette ball at my grandfather's unsuspecting legs. Doing Latin by correspondence was even worse than doing it at school: it was furtive, as well as nerdy. How was I going to explain that to Sophia? My entire family seemed intent on turning me into a geek before I even started at Pembroke.

❋

At my final piano lesson for the year, Mrs Sivan's lounge room was festooned with Christmas cards, as if a hundred multi-coloured birds had alighted there.

'You must be the most popular woman in Adelaide,' my father said.

'My students from *everywhere*,' she beamed. 'From Australia, from Russia, from America.'

I scanned the room for my Christmas card and found it on the mantelpiece by the window, beside a large vase of roses. *Dear Mrs Sivan*, I had written. *Merry Christmas and Happy New Year. From Anna G x.* I had hesitated at the 'from', wondering whether I should write 'love' instead. It seemed a bit forward, so I had kept it as it was, and added the x as compensation.

'Numbers not important,' she continued. 'More important is message from the heart. Here, I show you beautiful example, from Chang in Singapore.'

She selected a card from a central position on the heater: *Dear Mrs Sivan, I never forget our lessons. You gave me the gift of music, the gift of knowledge. It is a priceless gift, and I am forever grateful.*

She put the card back down. 'Unbelievable. After just two lessons – masterclasses, really. I like this expression – yes? – the gift of knowledge.' She turned to me. 'Gratitude *very* important. Not for me, I don't need, but for *you*. Important *always* to know your roots, and say thank you.'

My own Christmas card now seemed a meagre offering. It had a nice design on the front, though, of a Christmas angel. Objectively, it was still the better card.

'Of course, you are *very* fortunate girl. First of all, to have such family, so involved in everything you touch, and such aim of learning in your surroundings. I never knew such dedicated father, who comes to *every* one of his daughter's piano lessons. And whole family wonderful: incredible strong mother, and grandparents *hugely* supportive.'

I shrugged. My family was okay, if a little square. My mother had already bought me a pair of brown Roman sandals to wear to Pembroke, despite my advice to the contrary. *When everybody else has pongy feet, you'll thank me*, she had said, *even if you're nothing but an ingrate now.*

'And really you have even more to thank your grandfather,

for bringing you to me. Because now you have school! Enormous luck in some ways, but in large sense, I don't believe in luck, only in fate. What is school? It is wonderful sense of belonging, of being very comfortable, of having *roots*. It is *individual contact* with your teacher. And when you learn to love yourself like a gift of God – not like me, me, me and ego, but like a full respectable human being – then you can always say thank you.'

I nodded virtuously: I always said a polite 'thank you' at the end of our lessons.

'Of course, easy to say *thank you* like just good manners. But I don't understand empty politeness for politeness. Much more important is real manners, from cultivated heart.'

'Those are lovely roses,' I changed the subject. 'Over there by my card.'

'Beautiful, yes? Kate brought them. This girl so excited, so wants to learn, so *alive* and so open. Was about to stop piano – she came near to end, full stop. Unbelievable, really, how easy to lose talented people along the way. Now *enormous* improvement. We had *great* lesson on Beethoven.'

'I'd like to learn some Beethoven, too,' I said.

'Why my students so grateful? Because I am nice lady?'

'Yes?' I guessed.

'Not. Nice lady is not enough. Is because they want to learn, is because they want to *know*.'

She dropped her voice. 'Knowledge very important, yes?'

'Of course.' I was unnerved. Her musical clairvoyance allowed her to look at a score and read the secret meaning behind the notes; she seemed to have a similar ability to discern the dark truths of my pubescent soul.

'Knowledge is great power,' she said, 'is greatest happiness.'

I shot my father a warning glance, lest he say something about ignorance and bliss.

'Knowledge is your store,' she continued. 'Everything we talking about in general culture – on art, on *languages*, on literature, on theatre, on human beings – you use for your practical knowledge. It's not knowledge for exam and examiner. Not. It's knowledge for your existence and future and growing. It's like seeds, seeds, seeds, seeds.' She stood up from her chair, sprinkling imaginary seeds around the carpet. 'And after you water the seeds, and care for them, you have … what?'

She gestured around the room. All I could see were a hundred Christmas cards, lined up like recriminations.

'You have beautiful and incredible harvest!' She beamed, and took her exercise book off the piano, turning to a brand-new page.

Anna, 1986 she wrote across the top in pencil, in a large, authoritative cursive.

'Next year we do *huge* repertoire.'

'Beethoven?' I asked.

'Of course. But first Czerny. Czerny basically created the bridge from classic, and to romantic. If we talk Chopin is bible of the piano, Czerny is all foundation of its existence. We talk about school. Czerny incredibly great student of Beethoven. Of course, Beethoven not greatest teacher, because of his temperament, and only able to give to certain people. But *greatest* musician. And Czerny definitely great teacher, and taught Liszt, and then Leschetizky, and then all the others, and finally *you*.'

I smiled bashfully, as history swung its vast spotlight on me.

'Highest level of culture we call class. Class is school, and result is *incredible* simplicity. Simplicity without defence. It's not creating something just to *looks like*. But to be.'

For Christmas, I received the new Swatch watch I had requested, with a customised band in the Pembroke colours of blue and yellow. I admired the way it brought out my tan; it made me look like a real Pembroke girl. When school started in February, I kept my forearm displayed prominently, hoping to draw attention away from my Roman sandals. I followed Sophia through the schoolyard, volleying greetings to her friends, and to her friendly acquaintances, and to those whose category was yet to be decided: 'Hi Bec, hi Pip, hi Sarah.' With careful practice, I had refined my eastern-suburbs vowels, so that 'hi' began more like a 'har' before finding its way back to 'i'. As long as the conversation went no further, nobody would pick me as a scholarship winner.

Twice a week, the entire middle school congregated for chapel. I sat in the balcony with the training choir, in front of Evelyn Chua. As her reedy voice sang out from behind me, with its perfect intonation and relentless vibrato, I stared down at the six hundred adolescents below – the blue blazers of the girls, the green blazers of the boys – and felt a sort of vertigo. Occasionally a high-achieving student was asked to come out to the front and shake the vice-principal's hand; I prayed that it might never be me.

'Where did you get your tarn?' Bec Sharpe asked me one Thursday, as we filed out of chapel.

'I beg your pardon?'

'Your gorgeous tarn – where did you get it?'

Tan. We called it a tan in Nailsworth.

'In Kensington Gardens, by Sophia's pool,' I admitted, though I knew it would have been better to say the Whitsundays, or at the very least, *our shack at Victor*.

She threw back her blonde mane and carolled with laughter. 'You're so hilarious. It's just gorgeous.'

I was mystified. No matter how much I studied their code, it remained impenetrable. At lunchtime, the quadrangle was commandeered by Year 10 boys of alarming physicality, with an arsenal of insults for girls who got in their way: *cow, slut, fat bitch*. As their tennis balls ricocheted around, the quadrangle became as unpredictable as a pinball machine. I was terrified that a ball might seek me out and hit me. It was not the pain that I feared, so much as how I might react: the graceless way I would flinch, the secret such an unguarded moment would reveal about me.

'Going out this weekend?' Georgina asked, as we passed her in the quadrangle.

Did Sunday lunch at my grandparents' house qualify as going out?

'Got a few things on,' Sophia said.

A ball whizzed past us, and Georgina screamed with laughter. 'Go Ben!' The boy winked and returned to his game of handball. 'Very cute,' she said, 'but way too young. I mean, most of my friends are celebrating their eighteenths. I tell you, I have to stop drinking. Look at this potbelly! That's what alcohol does to you, girls.'

As she was talking, I heard rather than saw the telltale whoosh of the tennis ball, whirring towards us. It landed with a thunk between my thighs and lodged there, my treacherous skirt transformed into a catcher's mitt.

After a moment's astonishment, the boys started hooting.

'Hole in one!'

'Nice *snatch*!'

Ben ran towards me, laughing, his dazzling teeth glinting in the summer light. I retrieved the ball from between my legs as gracefully as I could and felt the blood rushing to my head. Did I return the ball to him over-arm and risk being accused of throwing like a girl? I settled on an under-arm lob, but released the ball too late and watched as it flew off above my head and disappeared backwards onto the library roof.

Ben's broad smile turned to a scowl. 'Stupid pig.'

Lucy quietly moved away.

'Why did you do that?' Sophia asked, as we walked alone to the grassed area.

❀

'Let us talk about woman and man,' Mrs Sivan said at our next lesson. 'Both have fantastic qualities. But sometimes man, even the biggest man, can look on the big picture and missing a lot of details. It's amazing way how.'

She turned to my father.

'Sorry, Peter. I not divide them artistically: both could be greatest artists. For example, Beethoven is *very* man composer.' She swung back to me. 'Of course, best of woman is *most* intelligent. But worst of woman can be terrible! She is *very* small. On the piano, she is very good at *knitting*. All details are superb. But no vision, no architectonic structure! If you have, for example, three days to go through forest, you can*not* stay two days in front of one tree. Impossible! Even if is most beautiful tree in the world. You must learn to manage your time better.'

She addressed me gravely. 'You, my darling, must be best of woman *and* best of man.'

Her coiffed hair surrounded her face like a halo; the soft clouds of her hands pressed against mine. Then she clenched my fist, and released it. 'Beethoven very masculine. And *very* demanding. He was so – how to explain? – unhappy with a lot of things and his surroundings. Very difficult, very frustrated, very *frustrating*. This type of person – what they fight, mostly? Other people? Not. They fight inside of themselves.'

She demonstrated a scale on the piano, each note blazing into the air.

'Is not Mozart, not.' She repeated the scale, invested with Mozartean song. 'More *defensive ego*. Beethoven is steely fingers. And altogether *huge aggressive attitude*.' She seized my upper arm with her fingertips. 'At the same time, his music is full of warmth, full of beauty, full of incredible possibilities of love. This is man with enormous heart, who was born artistical genius. What he needs? Love and support. But no woman to love him, not ever. Not mother, not wife. Loveless life. He *dream* about it.' She studied my face. 'Very difficult for child, yes, but you so clever girl. Of course I will never teach the last sonatas until you are ready. No need to jump over. But some Beethoven we can start immediately.'

She opened my edition of Beethoven's *Klavierstücke* and turned to the Rondo a Capriccio, 'Rage over a Lost Penny'.

'Mozart is opera – yes? Beethoven *always* orchestra. His hearing *completely* symphonic. In some ways, he loves orchestral instrument even better than *instrumentalist*. He loves orchestral instrument until it comes to life.'

She formed my left hand into the opening chord, and when I played, it summoned the sound of an orchestra into the room. I shook her hand off and tried to do it myself.

'Not. We need more *instrument* in sound. We don't play, we conduct. What is here? Tonic and dominant over tonic pedal. Little finger *insistent* on G. Beethoven *very* intellectual composer, for him harmony hugely important.'

She always pronounced harmony as *garmony*; it came to mean something more to me than mere harmony: something with narrative qualities, something emotionally charged.

'What is garmonic logic here?' she asked, and sketched it out for me at the piano, so that I had a bird's-eye perspective on the piece: its large argument, its architectonic structure. 'But logic alone not enough. Every sentence important, every word important. And not just word – *spelling* must be exact.'

My father jotted this down in his notebook.

'You must remember: music is big and beautiful forest. You see every little tree and enjoying, but *always* you remember big forest. *What!*' She threw her hands up in the air. 'This is master.'

I felt daunted; she was demanding no less than the omniscience of God.

'My darling, you exhausted,' she said, gently. 'Of course. Beethoven so intensive. He *eat* you.'

❋

At school, it was getting more difficult to conceal the fact that I was a brain. Sophia and I sat neither too close to the front, nor too close to the back of the class, and we had a strict policy of never putting up our hands. Occasionally a teacher directed a question towards me, and I had to speak. I didn't recognise the voice that rang out across the classroom: it had a strange, affected English accent; it knew too much.

At the Adelaide Eisteddfod that year, I failed to recapture my earlier honourable mention, which now seemed the freak triumph of a vanished youth; but at school, academic awards lobbed themselves promiscuously into my arms. I pretended not to care, and would have traded any of these prizes for eisteddfod success or greater popularity, but at home I took them out of my school bag and arranged them on the mantelpiece. There were plaques from the National Chemistry Quiz, the IBM State Mathematics Competition, the South Australian Young Writers Awards, the ESSO National Science Competition. Lined up next to each other, in my bedroom, they did look like a kind of popularity.

The biggest competition of the year was the Westpac Mathematics Competition, held in July. It was a multiple-choice exam, marked by computer; marks were deducted for wrong answers, forcing you to perform a separate, quiet mathematics of probability before guessing. As our teacher handed out the papers, I arranged my 2B pencil, pencil sharpener and eraser alongside my scribble paper, correcting the angles between them until they were exactly 90 degrees. When he handed me the exam paper, I positioned it at the exact centre of my desk. It was a mysterious, alluring document; I wondered what secrets it would reveal to me about myself.

'You may start,' he announced, and there was a loud whoosh of papers. I moved fast through the first section, applying my sharpened pencil to the plump whiteness of the answer form, colouring each answer into a perfect, tight oblong, so that the computer would have no reason to feel confused. As the exam proceeded, the questions became more difficult, until I had to read them several times before they made sense. I did not yet have the mathematical processes for these calculations, but I quietened down and let my mind reach out for them, waiting for what the questions told me *after*. There was such privacy in this place, such quietness; I felt as safe as within a piece of music. Outside, the quadrangle was blessedly free of boys and their balls, and the sun moved slowly across the sky at an angle mathematics could determine.

'Time's up,' the teacher said, and we surrendered our papers.

'That was a waste of time,' Georgina said, as we filed outside.

Sophia agreed, but this time I remained silent.

Some weeks later in chapel, after the first hymn, the vice-principal, Mr Inverarity, stood up to address the school.

'I've just received some wonderful news. One of our Year 8 students has brought prestige to herself and to the school community through her outstanding performance in the Westpac Mathematics Competition.'

The blood rushed to my face; I prayed that it was not me, and also that it was.

'I haven't yet had the chance to tell her personally, but Anna Goldsworthy was one of only three students in South Australia, from all year levels, to receive a medal. Are you here, Anna?'

I put up my hand.

'Yes, there you are, up in the choir stalls.'

The entire school swivelled around to stare at me.

'You're a long way back there, so I will ask you to come down now.'

I stood, grimly; being summoned to the front of chapel was my worst nightmare. *Don't trip, don't trip,* I muttered to myself, as I worked my way along the pew. Why was everybody murmuring? How could I know for sure that I didn't have a wedgie? As I approached the stairs, a Year Nine mezzo-soprano grabbed the arm of my blazer. 'What are you doing?' She yanked me down into the pew beside her. 'He said, "I *won't* ask you to come down now."'

The entire school erupted in laughter.

'Order,' called out Mr Inverarity. 'I'm sure you'll have further opportunities for public acknowledgment in chapel, Anna. But at this juncture, I only ask that we express our congratulations with a round of applause.'

At house athletics trials that afternoon, Sophia and I reported our hurdle results to the Year Nine sports captain, posted behind the table.

'Are you the brain?' he asked me.

My cover was blown; there was no point denying it.

'Yes,' I confessed, as Sophia gasped.

'Well, it's a good thing you can do maths,' he said, 'because you're fucking hopeless at hurdles.'

Chapter 6. Schubert

B ACK WHEN I WAS EIGHT YEARS OLD, my father had published his first two books, each with an unpronounceable name: a collection of stories, *Archipelagoes*, and a collection of poems, *Readings from Ecclesiastes*. At the Adelaide Writers' Week launch, my brother and I rolled deliriously down the grass hills while the grown-ups made speeches. Neither book made much sense to me – the poems didn't even rhyme – but I brought *Archipelagoes* into school for show and tell, to prove that my dad was famous.

Mrs Vaughan had sat me on her lap and begun reading the first story to the class: *It was no fun living next door to a home handyman – especially one like Evan who was so relentlessly efficient at it …*

'He should be an example to you!' my wife would say.

'He is!' I would answer. 'Of a real pain in the …'

She glanced at me over her glasses, disappointed. 'I think we'll say "a real pain in the leg".'

The class sniggered. She continued with less enthusiasm:

79

Hardly a day went by without my wife noticing fresh evidence of his handiwork.

'I see Evan is laying bricks in his drive,' she'd suggest pointedly.

'I don't care if he's laying the bloody Avon lady ...'

Mrs Vaughan snapped the book shut. 'That's enough for today,' she said brightly. 'Everybody give Anna a big clap for having such a clever daddy!'

Over the next five years, my father published a steady stream of poems and short stories, maintaining that they were purer forms of literature than the vastly overrated novel. But at home, he spent each morning huddled over our new Macintosh 128, working on a book about a mathematician called Claude. Gradually, drafts piled up to fill a cupboard, as the manuscript became human-sized, like a sixth member of the family. Occasionally he gave me the latest version to read. The story was set exclusively in a hotel room at the Adelaide Hilton International; at its climax, Claude undressed in front of a mirror and counted all the moles on his body. I didn't really get the point, but I went through the drafts with a pen, collecting inconsistencies and repetitions, as proof of my attentiveness. In an interview with the *Age*, he described me as his favourite editor. To be praised by my father in print astonished and delighted me; it was the highlight of my thirteenth year.

One Saturday morning, after returning home from my theory lesson, I wandered into his study.

'How's Claude?'

'I've got something else for you.' He scrolled to the top of a document. 'Have a look at this, Pie.'

He waggled a forefinger in front of my nose. It was our second lesson? Our third?

'*This finger is selfish. Greedy. A … a delinquent. He will steal from his four friends, cheat, lie.*'

'But what about Claude?' I asked.

'Don't worry about Claude. I'm just going to have a play with this for a while and see where it goes.'

I read on.

He sheathed the forefinger in his closed fist as if it were the fleshy blade of a Swiss army knife and released the middle finger.

'*Mr goody-goody,*' *he said, banging the finger down on middle C repeatedly.* '*Teacher's pet. Does what he is told. Our best student.*'

Last came the ring finger.

'*Likes to follow his best friend,*' *he told me.* '*Likes to … lean on him sometimes.*'

He lifted his elbows upwards and outwards.

'*Those are the pupils. This is the teacher. The elbow—*'

'You can't do this!' I cried out. I knew he drew from life in his writing, but this was worse. It was robbery. 'Have you even asked Mrs Sivan?'

'Don't worry, Pie, I'll show it to her when I finish it. *If* I finish it. People are usually flattered to inspire books.'

I ran out to the back garden to tell my mother. She let the lawnmower idle for a moment as she listened, squinting at me under her sun visor.

'Deary, deary, deary me,' she said, and then revved up the machine and finished her mowing.

At my next lesson I took Schubert's impromptus out of my music satchel and placed them on the music stand as if everything were normal and I was not part of a covert operation.

'What is the tragedy in Schubert?' Mrs Sivan asked. 'You

must remember two things: first of all, his intuition of death. Some sort of premonition that he will have death at a young age. On the other hand, he *so* happy to live. Like a young child, who will tell you he has cancer, for example, but he doesn't believe it, not completely. Mum or Dad or nice doctor will still save him. In some ways, tragedy not right word. More about asking *why*. Basically, sadness and acceptance and pain, and altogether light and innocence.' She took a tissue from the box at the piano and wiped her eyes. 'Always remember that Schubert is greatest song composer. Of course, you say, but what about Mozart?'

I nodded. Given time, I might have asked this question.

'Not! Mozart is opera, and there is nothing opera in Schubert. Only song. Why? Because song so intimate. *Every* sound very personal. Only your own voice can be here.' Her face darkened. 'I tell you one thing: Schubert never, ever lie. He *lives* in his music: all his world, all his love, all his life, is here.' She leant back in her chair, to address both my father and myself. 'Of course, liar cannot play piano. Impossible. With words we can find ways to cover, but with sounds, not. And sometimes not necessary to lie. Sometimes enough to *say nothing*.'

I shot a panicky look at my father.

'Very important to have foundation of morals. If you lie, your sounds will be killed *immediately!*' She turned back to me. 'You are lucky girl, by the way, to have such interested father taking notes.' I glared at my father, willing him to confess, but he continued his transcribing.

'Schubert by nature completely romantic, but with Beethoven's touch. Of course he very impressed by Beethoven, and copies him, but his inside world *incredibly* different. If Beethoven was fighter, constantly, and sometimes against the whole world, Schubert will surrender before he even starts to fight.' She took my finger and drew a Schubert sound from the piano. 'Is like you take needle, injection.' There was so much sweetness in it, alongside something else, something darker. 'Altogether Schubert is a *million* times more romantic than Beethoven, and a *million* times kinder. He is clear romantic in skin and heart and everything, but form and structure all classical.' She turned to the Impromptu in A Flat. 'We begin with A-flat minor chord. Listen, don't play. The inside story of this garmonic chord is incredible: its emotional story. And altogether we must think about pulse, and about hearing volume.'

Her sounds beckoned to me; they came in and out of focus. I wanted to find my way into her world, but I couldn't quite get there. At the end of the lesson, when she guided me to the door, I could see from her face that it was as taxing for her as it was for me. 'Promise me this week you will try to listen, my darling, yes? Playing the piano must be as natural as speaking. Speaking is not about moving your mouth and – what is it? – *tongue!* Not! Is about communicating visions.'

I promised her I would try to listen, but at home I couldn't remember how. It was easier just to play, so I thundered wildly, heedlessly through the trio section of the impromptu, repeating it over and over again until my forearms hurt and I wept with pity for myself and for Schubert.

'Not,' she said the following week. 'Schubert never sentimental. No way.' She showed me back to his sound: to that exquisite realm he occupied between major and minor, and it was here that I wished to remain, away from the lies and half-truths and omissions of the outside world.

❊

At school, I had abandoned my dream to be a Pembroke girl, and instead cultivated the persona of artiste. I wandered dreamily through the quadrangle, with my head cocked to one side as if struck by inspiration, keeping a wary eye out for tennis balls. This was only partly affectation. I played music constantly in my imagination: it had become my anaesthetic, a protective gauze through which I experienced the world. Its harmonies sweetened the dissonances of adolescence: that three boys in our year had been suspended for trafficking marijuana, which turned out, on closer inspection, to be a mixture of lavender and rosemary; that Nina had given Sam a blow job at a party on the weekend.

'Why is it called a blow job?' I asked Sophia at recess. We sat on the lawn, eating packets of Nutella from the tuckshop with dainty white spoons. 'Did she actually blow?'

She shrugged. 'I don't think so.'

We ate in silence for a moment, while I tried to think of something else to say. We had already revised yesterday's conversations, and fine-tuned our responses of surprise or derision.

'My dad has a new collection of stories coming out later this year,' I remembered. 'And he's just been invited to be writer-in-residence at Brisbane Grammar at the beginning of third term.'

'We all have dads you know,' she said. 'We just don't all talk about them all the time.'

I stared at a blade of grass. After a moment, the G-flat Major Impromptu started up in my head; when it was finished, recess was over.

'Schubert in some ways was most unluckiest composer,' Mrs Sivan said. 'Unlucky with life: no money, no fame, no recognition. Of course, he had vision of his music's future: he knew it would be immortal. But at the same time, this is very interesting, he had no ego. Everyone singing his songs, but no-one knowing who he is. And the only date he has concert, what happens?'

'What?'

'The great violinist Paganini comes to Vienna! And of course *everyone* goes to Paganini's concert. All public, all critics. And one other thing ...' She dropped her voice. 'Not very right to say, perhaps, but he was very *unbeautiful* man.'

I was learning about unbeautiful. Puberty had not only vandalised my face with acne, but seemed to have disassembled my body and put it back together all wrong. I had always been tall, but now I had become outrageously tall, well beyond the limits of good taste. Cars no longer tooted as I hunched along the street; at night, I undressed hastily with my eyes averted, so that I didn't have to acknowledge what had become of my child's body: those ballooning thighs, these sudden hips, the way they insisted on a womanliness I was not prepared for.

My mother took me to her expensive hairdresser, who styled my hair in a Liza Minnelli cut, tapering to wisps beneath my ears: an extravagant frame for my acne-ridden face. My grandmother knitted me a smart jumper, in forest-green. 'Stand up straight and look people confidently in the eye,' she instructed. 'And that's half the battle already won.' My father showed me a speech he had written for the launch of a new collection of short stories. I took out my pen and went hunting eagerly for corrections, until I came to a line:

My current theory is that acne serves a useful evolutionary purpose. It renders adolescent children distasteful to their parents, and so makes the pain of separation easier to bear.

I handed it back to him, unmarked. 'It's a good speech,' I told him. Later that night, I asked my mother if she might speak to him about it. I wasn't hurt, of course. I was bigger than that: even the *Age* knew I was his favourite editor. It was just that it might be embarrassing for everyone if the line was delivered at the launch while his daughter stood beside him.

'It's only a joke, Pie,' he said, when he came into my bedroom to say goodnight. 'No-one will take it seriously. It's just one of the great lines.'

At the launch, he delivered the line and there was a smattering of laughter. Nobody looked at me, but I felt myself blush redder behind my acne.

❋

Over the next month, my father's preliminary sketches about fingers started taking shape as a novel while Claude remained in the cupboard, untended.

'A novel is never finished,' he explained. 'Only at some stage abandoned.'

Sometimes, on weekends, I accompanied him to the Barr Smith Library at the University of Adelaide, to research the Leschetizky school. I would happily have spent all my time there, in the dusty half-light of Dewey Decimal System 786.2, poring over books with my father. In this corner of the world, playing the piano was not an obscure geekish activity, but everyone's central concern.

We borrowed a handful of books, including Harold C. Schonberg's *The Great Pianists*. I was enchanted by Schonberg's easy, confidential tone, his gossipy asides, as though these legendary pianists were our mutual friends. I devoured his pages on Leschetizky, who emphasised relaxation at the piano, or 'devitalizing ... the muscles not called into place'. Artur Schnabel recalled that Leschetizky insisted on 'truthfulness of expression, and he would not tolerate any violation or deviation from what he felt to be true'. I remembered Mrs Sivan's words – *liar cannot play piano* – and felt myself piecing together an inheritance.

At school, I gazed out of the window in maths, wishing I was in the Barr Smith Library. There was a small string of raindrops hanging like beads along a tree branch. I thought of pearly legato, and of Annette Essipoff, who had taught Mrs Sivan's professor, with her 'cat-like strength and poise'. Did that sound like me? Or did I more closely resemble the legendary Teresa Carreño, who was 'talented, temperamental, tempestuous and beautiful'?

'Hello!' repeated the boy sitting in front of me.

I jumped in my chair.

'I think you're actually the most boring person I've ever met,' he said.

I gaped back at him; I had no rebuttal.

Often when we arrived at lessons, Kate Stevens was there already. Mrs Sivan sang along as she played, grabbing her hands and repositioning them, her cheeks flushed with delight, demonstrating a different sound, a changed inflection. Sitting on that couch, at one remove from the keyboard, I could understand better what she was asking for; I could hear the eloquence and specificity of each of her sounds.

'Exactly! And now this F has ambition to go where?'

Kate never seemed discouraged by correction: 'To B flat.'

'Of course. Much better, but now not enough hearing left hand. Left hand needs to be more distant, more isolated. It's not that she's not involved, but she's afraid to touch the person in case she destroys him.' She swung around to address my father. 'Sometimes, you know, too much help can be destructive.'

Kate tried again.

'Excellent!' Mrs Sivan called out, spinning back to her. 'Always we have two ways in our development, yes?'

'Yes,' Kate said. 'Slave or master.'

'Of course. In slavery, we can reach the absolute peak of decoration and information, and do it perfect, like a lot of pianists. But master is like you open new sluices out of your body. You have another breath. Master gives you visions.'

At the end of the lesson, Kate stood up and peeled her skirt from the back of her thighs. 'We've been working for four hours without a break,' she grinned.

'What, so long?' asked Mrs Sivan. 'But of course, easy to forget about time when working. So enjoyable.'

She showed Kate to the door, and I moved to the piano stool, hoping that my newfound perspective on sound would not desert me. But sitting here, in front of the keyboard, I felt dazzled again by the promise of *playing* an instrument and achieving a sound. I launched into the Schubert Impromptu in A Flat.

'Not,' Mrs Sivan called out, as she returned. 'You playing, not hearing. We want *up* sound here – you must liberate little finger.'

I persisted through her corrections, as Kate might.

'Not, this accent different. Always listening to volume, always listening to *inside pulse*.'

For a moment I understood her meaning and caught the pulse of the semiquavers like a wave. I felt the freedom of 'inside hearing': the astonishing dissolution of technical problems through a slight change in perspective, a different way of listening.

'Exactly! Not playing. You start with ingredients of science, and you make beautiful *cake* of arts. Promise me, darling, that you will try to listen this week. No playing, only hearing.'

I promised, but at home, away from the illumination of her teaching, my playing once more became prosaic, mechanical. Frustrated, I closed the piano and picked up *The Great Pianists*.

Among [Leschetizky's] strictures was the falsity of the concept that long hours of practice were beneficial. He would not think of a student working six, seven, eight hours a day. 'No-one can do that without being mechanical, and that's just what I'm not interested in. Two hours, or three at most, is all anyone should require if he will only listen to what he is playing and criticise every note.

Perhaps, by extension, two to three hours were not necessary, and thirty minutes would suffice, with the right intention. Just for today, and perhaps tomorrow, I would read about the piano instead of practising. If I concentrated hard enough, I might be able to read my way to becoming a concert pianist.

Chapter 7. Mozart

OVER THE YEARS, as I sat beside Mrs Sivan at her piano, the room around us gradually transformed. First, the iridescent pink of the wall gave way to a more tasteful cream; later, the battered walnut piano swelled into a Yamaha grand. Each year, the army of miniature pianos on the bookshelf grew in ranks, until it occupied the shelves below; and finally the room itself expanded, acquiring new carpet and two small chandeliers. Other things remained constant: a geometric red clock that I snuck peeks at when exhausted; a daguerreotype of Chopin over the mantelpiece; and, above the piano, a photograph of Mrs Sivan as an eighteen-year-old at an international competition. She had the alabaster skin of a film star, and surveyed the room with ferocious, queenly eyes.

'The stage must be like another room in your house,' she often reminded me, and as I sat my piano exams in her living room each year, I began to understand this. Despite the surreal presence of the examiner, slurping tea at a bridge table, there were those toy pianos standing by, like small familiars, and my regal teacher overseeing proceedings from her position on the wall. I skipped the exams she deemed unnecessary – 'we do exams *by the way* only' – and hopscotched between A and A-plus, until at age thirteen I found myself in Eighth Grade, with only one exam remaining before the celestial realm of the Associate Diploma.

Eighth Grade was a serious exam, demanding proficiency in every scale, and an official venue: the Flinders Street School of Music. It was cold and dark in there on a Saturday afternoon, and I missed my miniature pianos and the dappled light of Mrs Sivan's chandeliers. Other candidates bustled around with their music satchels, or practised behind closed doors. I had a cold, and had to keep stopping to blow my nose as my father sat beside me in a practice room, testing my scales: 'A-flat melodic minor in sixths, *staccato.*'

Usually I could see the whole scale before I started: its particular topography, its imprint on the keyboard. But in these intimidating surroundings, my mental map vanished, and I launched into the scale at ground level, faltering around F and G. I tried again, and came unstuck on the way down. My father tugged anxiously at his Adam's apple.

'Can you please stop doing that?' I asked.

He released the skin between his fingers and it pinged back into his neck.

An official knocked on the door: 'The examiner is ready for you, Miss Goldsworthy.'

I closed the piano and followed him to the recital room, where he opened the large swing doors. 'Break a leg, Pie,' my father whispered. There was a crinkled ridge of skin on his neck, where it had surrendered its elasticity. All my vulnerability was there; I turned away, and stepped into the exam.

The examiner was a heavy man in half-moon glasses, planted solidly behind a vinyl table, as unbudgeable as the Bösendorfer grand which stood before me. I knew he was an organist, which seemed a good sign, as I had frequently been complimented on my Bach.

'Make yourself comfortable,' he grunted, and returned to his papers.

I sat down at this unfamiliar instrument. It had four extra bass notes, coloured black, which veered up towards me, vertiginously.

'When you're ready.'

As soon as I began the Bach prelude and fugue, my nose began to run. I scanned the bars ahead for handkerchief opportunities, but the only chance was before the fugue.

'Thank you,' he said tersely, when I had finished.

I blew my nose and then stared at the keyboard, aware that I had to salvage things with the Mozart. *Mozart's life season is always spring. What is it spring in our life? Hope. Blossom. Expectation. The first face of the leaves of life. And Mozart full of it!*

It was difficult to imagine spring in the cold winter of this building, but I invested my sounds with as much joy as I could summon, and they amplified it and returned it to me, and at the end of the movement my cold seemed to have vanished. I performed the Schubert and Copland, exhilarated by the redemptive powers of music, while the examiner stared over his glasses. Afterwards, he asked for very few scales, and nodded abruptly to say the exam was finished.

I exploded out the swing doors to join my father. 'Seemed a jolly fellow,' I told him.

The following Wednesday, I returned home from choir practice to find an unopened envelope waiting for me on the kitchen bench. My father emerged from his bedroom, where he had been packing for a poetry conference in Malaysia. 'Letter for you!'

I went to the fridge and poured myself a glass of orange juice.

'Going to open it?' my mother asked.

Why did my parents have to be so *nosey*? I snatched the envelope up and took it into the dining room. It was important to open it with a great deal of precision, so as not to affect the result within, so I pushed the chairs in evenly around the table, and drank my orange juice in exactly eleven sips, a prime number. I positioned the envelope in the centre of the table, a small rectangle in perfect parallel to a larger one, and prepared myself for the opening. Of course, an A-plus would be ideal, but I had resolved not to be disappointed by an A. Still, my heart was pounding as I eased the envelope open and slid out the semi-transparent paper of my report.

I didn't hear myself scream, but my parents came bursting into the room like superheroes.

Sitting in the box in the lower left-hand corner was the result, written in a giant, toad-like sprawl: C.

'You've got to be fucking joking!' my father exclaimed. He double-checked my name on the front of the envelope, and double-checked my candidate number. But that was my repertoire listed in the left-hand column – Bach, Mozart, Schubert, Copland – alongside an unrecognisable vocabulary: *disappoint-*

ing, in need of improvement, not altogether successful. I studied the C, wondering if it could be a very messy sideways A, but it remained resolutely, corpulently C-like, until it conflated in my mind with the examiner and I found it difficult to breathe, as if sat on by both man and result.

'Now, darling, it's just one man's opinion,' my mother said, putting her arm around my shoulder.

I brushed her away: didn't she know anything? A C grade was still, nominally, a pass; but in order to sit my Associate Diploma I had to receive a B at least – a depth to which I had never imagined sinking. This C was a ban on going any further, a sentence imposed by an institution as formidable as any law court in the country: the Australian Musical Examinations Board. I had known disappointment at the eisteddfods, but it had never been scandalous disappointment: it was no great disgrace to be one of thirty contestants who did not receive a prize. But here, I had been singled out by failure, branded personally with a C, and forever. I started to sob, as my siblings' anxious faces hovered at the panes of the French doors.

'This is bullshit,' my father said, pacing the room. 'Utter corrupt bullshit. If I come across that examiner in a dark alley in Kuala Lumpur, I'll teach him a thing or two.'

I stopped weeping for a moment to gauge how much consolation I could take from this. Not much; I resumed my crying. But even through my shock, I recognised something inevitable about this C, something deserved. It clanged like a gong, backwards and forwards in time, picking up resonances from the past – *Anna will not be concert pianist, not* – and providing a pedal note, a giant fundamental, for all the failures that might follow.

'Of course is impossible,' Mrs Sivan said, when I showed her the report at my next lesson. 'When you called me, I was stunned. But I tell you, my darling, is best lesson really: you can never depend on results.' She took the report from my hands and scanned through it. 'Altogether, is not malicious man. Not at all. Just organist, and does not understand the piano. What is this – "disappointingly facile"?'

'He thought my Mozart sounded too easy, too glib.'

'Exactly!' she declared, triumphantly. 'This says *everything*. Does not understand Mozart at all, wants you to play like on organ.'

She launched into the opening of the Mozart sonata, sat-irising the heavy-handed approach of an organist. Then she segued into her own irresistible reading, shining with life, and my failure danced away, momentarily exorcised through song.

'This is Mozart,' she laughed. 'Mozart is absolutely human being, and in love first of all with the human, with people around him! And of course his favourite is young soprano, *leggiero* soprano – why? Because it is reminding him of little blossom, beginning to flower, beginning to bloom. Of course your father very angry, and want to write letter. But I told him: why make unnecessarily enemy? Better we do exam again next year. Will be *peanuts* for you, my darling. Alto-gether we do *huge explosion* of repertoire. And at the concert next week, you will play beautifully, and show them face of Mozart.'

A week later, I climbed reluctantly onto the stage for the rehearsal at Elder Hall. *Back on the horse*, I told myself, *Giddy-up*. There was only a scattering of students present, and the empty plush red seats stared back at me like a silent jury. Every sound I pitched into the cavernous space carried an extra freight of self-doubt, and bounced on the empty seats and vanished into the carpet. I waited for Mrs Sivan to come onstage and correct me, but she remained in the audience, clapping politely when I approached.

'Altogether, not so bad,' she said. 'More hearing, of course, less playing. For example, is impossible to sit here at end of phrase. Remember always punctuation.' She demonstrated by playing on her lap, her hands dimpling like a baby's, her eyes shining with the return of music.

'Mozart has so many ranges of smiling. Despite all tragedy of his life, Mozart is incredibly optimistic. Why? Because his life itself is love. Most important, that you enjoy being onstage. That you love sharing your music.' I realised she was being gentle on me, and felt a renewed shame and started to cry. She stood to address the auditorium. 'Anna has had greatest lesson. I told: *greatest!* Always your music coming inside and growing. Much more important than instant results.' She flung her arms around me and kissed my hair. 'How I love this girl!'

Her students applauded, merciless in their pity. I excused myself and ran outside to wait for my mother on North Terrace. Someone came running after me, and I turned to see Kate Stevens, the sun catching on her gold hoop earrings. She had just finished her final school exams and seemed to have shed her schoolgirlness overnight, becoming larger and more radiant.

'How are you?' she asked.

'Fine.'

She walked beside me for a moment in silence. 'I heard about the exam. I don't know what to say, except that it's ridiculous.'

'Don't worry about it. I don't care, anyway.'

'That's wise. Like Mrs Sivan says, you can never depend on results.'

I wondered if I might be able to believe this after all. 'How did your school exams go?'

She grinned, broadly. 'Well, they're over! Now I'm free to practise as much as I want!'

'How much practice do you do, anyway?'

She dropped her voice. 'While I was at school, I could only manage four hours. Having all day at the piano is bliss.'

I thought about this. 'Do you have a grand piano?'

'Yes, but I'm not sure that makes much difference. Your Mozart was beautiful, by the way. Break a leg tomorrow night.'

She ran back to the rehearsal, her long hair streaming behind her like a flame. I watched her disappear into the giant mausoleum of Elder Hall and twisted a sideburn of hair between my fingers, willing it to grow faster.

It shocked me that Kate did so much practice. Didn't she know Leschetizky's views on the subject? Wasn't she worried about becoming mechanical?

'Is everything all right?' my mother asked, as I mulled this over in the car. But Kate's playing was far from mechanical. It was free and reckless and exhilarating. 'How was the rehearsal?' Both of my parents had been irritatingly solicitous since the exam.

'Fine.'

Of course, Mrs Sivan had suggested two hours' practice a day when I started learning from her, but I had come to believe that amount of time was something aspirational, a life-long maximum. Increasingly, I spent my practice sessions reading about music. Earlier that week, I had come across a passage on practice by the pianist Louis Kentner:

Pianists can be divided into the following three categories: those who practise a lot and admit it; those who practise a lot but deny it; and those who do not practise and, therefore, are not pianists.

I dismissed this as misguided. With the greater authority of Leschetizky behind me, I knew better.

But what if Kentner was right?

Mrs Sivan never insisted I practise more. Instead, she guided me patiently through the same lessons each week, entreating me to try to listen. And over the five years I had been with her, my playing had certainly improved. I had assumed that it would now develop into something like Kate's, of its own accord: that my technique would sprout octaves, as inevitable as puberty. If you wanted something enough, you would get it. Wasn't that how it worked? Anyway, hadn't I already sacrificed enough for my dream? Hadn't I sacrificed my popularity?

But when we returned home, I ignored the summons of the bookshelves, and my mother's offer of a cup of tea, and went straight to the piano, to practise for an hour and a half before dinner. I worked carefully through the Mozart, willing myself to remember what Mrs Sivan had said about sitting, about punctuation.

At dinner, I polished off my dessert. 'Could I please leave the table?'

'You're working hard,' my mother remarked.

'You find that you have to,' I explained, patiently. 'Kate practised four hours a day when she was at school. But of course she has a grand piano, which makes it easier.'

I sensed an exchange of looks – that click of parental complicity – and felt ashamed.

'When I sell the movie rights to my novel, we'll get a grand piano,' my father offered.

'We'll have to move into a bigger house,' my mother said. 'Something like that villa in Edward Street. Then there'll be room for all sorts of things that we want.'

'An indoor BMX track,' suggested my brother.

'A rabbit!' my sister whispered.

Over the course of that week, my feelings of failure were replaced by a sense of martyrdom, and then by a fierce resolve. I decided there was no way I would let *them* stop me, whoever they might be. Backstage at Elder Hall on Friday night, as I listened to the hum of the audience, I prepared to show them the face of Mozart. When I stepped out onto the stage, I saw my parents and my brother and sister and both sets of my grandparents occupying almost an entire row, their faces bursting with encouragement. Under the fierce floodlight of their support, I could see my own heroism, and felt moved by it.

But as I started to play, what I felt was not righteousness, but an inexplicable joy. I felt so many ranges of smiling: that this was a concert and not an exam; that Christmas was coming and I would have the holidays to practise; that my irritating but supportive family was here for me, in the audience; and that I was up on this stage, playing Mozart, who turned everything he touched into song. I allowed this joy into my sounds, which no longer crashed to the ground, self-defeated, but reached out into the audience in thanksgiving, saying things otherwise unavailable to my adolescent self.

It was no definitive Mozart, but nor was it the Mozart of an organist. And if Elder Hall was not yet a room in my house, nor was it a mausoleum. It felt instead like a gigantic ark, in which all the important species were accounted for; perhaps we could stay here forever, afloat on these sounds.

Chapter 8. Chopin

'WE HAVE EXCELLENT NEWS!' Mrs Sivan announced at my next lesson. 'Kate has been awarded prize for Year 12 exam. Not just for best pianist – not! Best of all instruments in all South Australia.'

'Congratulations,' said my father. 'That's wonderful.'

'Not just wonderful: *fantastic.* This is girl who came almost to full stop. Everybody telling her to play violin, not piano. But she has great will: *so* wants to learn. And we made huge shock.'

She turned to me. 'Next we make huge shock with Anna. I could see immediately at the concert: Anna also has this *fighting spirit.* Of course, must do enormous work. We must start études Chopin *immediately.*' She searched through a pile of scores on her piano until she found a battered beige book, with orange Cyrillic letters across the front, and placed it reverently on the music stand. 'Chopin études is most important book in life, but like the Bible, three-quarters of people don't understand what's written in it. In Chopin this is even more dangerous, because all secrets written in sounds. You have to have enough brain to understand, but what else?'

'Enough heart?'

'Of course enough heart! And enough knowledge and intuition and special pianistic levels. These études are *encyclopaedia* of virtuosity. Impossible to play mechanical, because *immediately* will be pain.' She dropped her voice. 'Even my first teacher, in Russia, wanted me to play like this, with butterfly technique.' She launched into an étude, labouring exaggeratedly with her arms. 'I have small hands, and feel pain immediately. My teacher said *pain is normal, don't worry!*'

'What did you do?' I asked.

She stretched out her hands in front of her, considering them. 'I will not say small hands are biggest gift from God. But *much* better than small brain!' She laughed. 'I ask her: "If Chopin études are greatest monument to pain, what is your point? That Chopin is masochist – yes? Or just sadist?"'

My father guffawed. 'What was her response?'

'She said, "Don't put this in your head." Always they tell me this. But I knew secret of no pain was already here, contained in étude. And then when I was eighteen, I met my professor, and I was amazed by her pianism. Such economy, such visions! She puts hand on the piano, just like this, so concentrated, so compact, and absolute depth of belonging.' She let her hand sink into the keyboard, hugging a handful of notes, their sounds rising to meet her like a choir. 'All sounds here. I recognise *exactly* what I have been looking for. She learned from Annette Essipoff, by the way. Of course she didn't want me as student.'

'Why not?'

She gazed out of the window.

'That's another story. Still she understands piano *incredibly*. These études are key to unlimited technical freedom. Here we have first étude, traditionally the most difficult.'

She launched into the opening page, the great bass octaves ringing through the room, her tiny right hand consuming massive stretches, effortless as a snake accommodating its prey. 'All secret is in position, and in hearing, and in listening to *pulse inside*.'

Then she turned to the second étude. 'And here, very tips of fingers, so precise, so delicate like ballet dancer, *en pointe*.' She performed the opening with an aerial lightness, her fourth and fifth fingers enacting a flawless chromatic scale.

'And number three, so personal and yet so objective. Chopin always talking about emotional response, which absolutely everyone has and can recognise. But his own particular experience, behind this response, is secret. This is the mystique of his music. He has a lot of love, but who he loves and how he loves – this is again secrecy.'

She played the opening. 'I can change my interpretation one hundred times, depends on how I feel today. Could be nostalgic, could be more innocent, could be – what is this? – idealistic ... This is freedom! But objective things, never change. We talked about woman and man, about big picture and little details. Chopin absolutely *epitome* of all little details working for big vision.'

She turned back to the contents page, circling five études I would begin with. 'Of course, eventually you must know all, because pianist without Chopin études does not exist.

Definitely you can't play them when in kindergarten or in first years of primary school. This is *peak* of virtuosity.'

Inspired, I spent the summer holidays practising Chopin instead of sunbaking by Sophia's pool. I no longer rattled through my practice deliriously, but carefully analysed each étude, reminding myself of Mrs Sivan's teachings, trying to trust my hands, to teach myself to hear. 'Every note is important,' she repeated, and if I noticed myself losing concentration, I would start again, fixing my mind on every sound, as in a meditation.

Practice, I discovered, had an addictive quality, beyond the unlocking of Chopin's secrets. It allowed me to be as obsessive-compulsive as I liked: to rehearse a mental process not just once, but again and again and again. 'It is not enough to understand,' Mrs Sivan told me, 'must *secure*. And one hundred per cent security not enough. Onstage, must be two hundred per cent at least.'

Slowly, practice became a physical need, without which I felt fidgety, unmoored; my four hours' practice mapped out a necessary personal space in the day. This became particularly important during the holidays, when my mother took time off work. I was seldom enlisted in chores if sitting at the piano. Repetitions of passagework shielded me from the sounds of her relentless industry: the throb of the lawnmower, the clanging of saucepans, the battle cries that announced an assault on the linen press. Somewhere, my brother began his clarinet practice, and then abandoned it. I would emerge from the study at the end of an afternoon to find that the compost had been mulched, a television cabinet built from scratch, and a tray of freshly baked rock buns was steaming on the bench.

'What shall we do next?' asked my mother.

My brother was lying on the sofa, looking post-traumatic.

'I'd better get back to work,' I said, taking a bun and retreating to the study.

'Guess how many hours' practice I did today?' I asked at dinnertime.

'Eight?' my mother asked.

'Infinity squared?' offered my brother.

'Five!' I announced, though it no longer sounded so impressive.

One weekend, my father took me to Festival Music, 'just to have a look at the grand pianos'. I moved from piano to piano, playing Chopin's Fifth Étude until the end of the first page, which was as far as I had memorised.

The salesman hovered nearby. 'You're clearly looking for a serious instrument.'

'Just browsing, thank you.'

'This one's a beauty, she is. Straight from Japan, where she's been *factory reconditioned*. Good as new, or should I say better than new. Been broken in at a music school. Saves you having to loosen her up yourself.'

I began the étude again. Playing it on this instrument amplified its brilliance, and other customers turned to look. Now that I had a captive audience, I wished I could play the whole thing, but I petered out at the end of the first page and sighed ostentatiously, as if disappointed by the piano.

'It's not quite right.'

The piano looked a little hurt behind its wide grin, but

I refused to feel guilty, since we were only playing make-believe.

'How is Chopin?' Mrs Sivan asked at my next lesson.

'Great,' I said.

'Of course Chopin great! Greatest in three: greatest composer, greatest pianist, greatest teacher.' I sat down at the piano, ready to demonstrate my progress with the Fifth Étude.

'Not!' she called out, as I started. 'No playing, only flying. Here we have – how do you say? – shaking out.' She demonstrated the crystalline opening, each finger as independent as a jumping bean. Then she grasped my hand and made it dance for her on the black keys. 'And here we have clapping, and now sprinkling, and now dancing.' As she manipulated my hand like a marionette, my fingers caught the impulse from within, and took flight.

'Exactly! Variety of choreography *endless*. Not one ballet dancer uses so many varieties as in these études. Basically, you dance your fantasy. This is completely new technique. I tell you: Chopin *greatest* teacher. How do I know?'

'He produced great students?'

'Not at all! Only taught members of aristocracy, because needed money. But all evidence here, in every detail of these études.' She leant back in her chair. 'Only one condition: *if*.'

'If what?'

'If you know how to read them. Then you have clear lesson with Chopin.'

I stared at the score, willing myself to read between the lines, but all I could see were the notes on the page, supplemented by the occasional instruction: *brillante, legato, crescendo.*

'How did you get your professor to teach you?' I asked, changing the subject.

She appraised me for a moment. 'Always I have good logic, like you. I said to her: I do not expect you to take me. I only want to play for you first. Better reject *after,* not before.'

'And she accepted you.'

She turned my hand upside down, examining it like a book. 'I could read her hands, and translate to other students. This, by the way, is how I learned I had teaching gift.'

※

At the beginning of Year 10, my housemistress, Mrs Athersmith, appointed me a prefect. This pleased me, as she was the schoolteacher I respected above all others, but I refused to be distracted by the honour. I had to conserve my energy for my true task, which was nothing less than the entire renovation of myself to create a concert pianist. Music became a justification for shyness, and I cultivated my silence like a spell. I submerged more and more deeply into practice, leaving my peers outside in the sunlight, without me.

Each Saturday morning, when I returned home from my theory lesson, I donned my practice uniform of navy tracksuit pants, red windcheater and Ugg boots. 'You really should branch out into some other outfit,' suggested my seven-year-old cousin. Sometimes my mother coaxed me into joining her at open-house inspections, and I was forced to change. Every weekend, for as long as I could remember, she had migrated back to the eastern suburbs of her childhood, zipping between properties for sale in Kensington Gardens and Norwood. It was an effort I supported in principle: a move to the eastern suburbs would minimise my travel time to school, freeing up more hours for practice. But over the years, as we failed to make an offer on anything, I came to suspect that these inspections were purely recreational.

Between properties, we stopped off for tea with my grandmother and my aunt, and my mother produced her stash of floor plans like enemy intelligence: 'Have a stickybeak at this!'

They pored over them on my aunt's kitchen bench, piecing together the neighbourhood.

'Love a plurry duck!' exclaimed my grandmother.

'They've gone and blocked out all that lovely northern light!' lamented my aunt.

The three of them clucked and shook their heads, and then my mother and I returned to the car, to collect further violations of common sense and good taste.

Now that my weekends were earmarked for work, I begrudged these hours in my mother's car, prisoner to her erratic gear changes, as the day's available practice time dwindled to nothing. One Saturday, I declared I would no longer accompany her to look at houses. I had serious work to do, and limited time for make-believe. After lunch, she knocked on the dining-room door to tell me she was going to an open inspection in Prospect.

'Who's going?'

'The whole family, but I know you don't have time. Ta-ta!'

I asked her to wait while I changed my outfit. Prospect was only a few blocks away; if necessary, I could escape on foot.

'What a waste of time,' I sighed, when we were crammed in

the car. 'I don't know why we're bothering. Prospect's further away from Pembroke!'

We swung into Rose Street and parked alongside a large Federation villa, and Pembroke no longer seemed so important.

'It's gi-normous,' my sister gasped.

We entered through its vast front door and hovered in the entrance foyer, overwhelmed by the stained glass.

'Come on then!' My mother marched ahead. 'No dilly-dallying!'

She led us through its passageways until we came to a living room with a large bay window. 'Now that,' she said, resonantly, 'would be perfect for a grand piano.'

My family moved into another room, but I stayed there, struck by the rightness of my mother's words. This bay window was not just perfect for a grand piano: it needed one. And if it had a piano, it would also need a pianist. I had a vision, which struck with the force of a prophecy: myself in that bay window, seated at the grand piano from Festival Music, practising Chopin études. As other potential buyers drifted in and out of the room, I surreptitiously touched every window and wall, tapped eleven times on the mantelpiece, and flicked the light switch quickly off and on again in order to make it happen.

'I tell you secret about Chopin,' Mrs Sivan confided in me. 'Piano is his best friend. More. He tells piano all his secrets. He put hand on the piano like this.'

I braced myself as she reached for my shoulder, but her touch was warm and affectionate.

'Enormous trust. No resistance: nothing between himself and piano. More than that, even.' She transferred her touch to the keyboard. 'Hands completely melted down. He *embrace* the piano.'

She dropped her voice and glanced around the room. 'In my opinion, George Sand not the true love of Chopin's life. This is. This instrument. Even he feel *physical* love for it. We have this absolute incredible – how do you say? – intimate physical knowing. In Chopin, the what and the how are one, not two. Not one mechanical sound ever. Will kill Chopin *immediately*. Once more, this middle section.'

I concentrated on embracing the piano, as I played the middle section of the Étude op. 25, no. 5. She took my left hand and guided it through the cello melody. 'Relax here,' she said, isolating a point at the bottom of my palm, and I felt the relief of letting go, so that my hand was kneading, not playing, and the sound it drew from the piano was pliable as dough.

'Chopin is Romantic who come into your body and into your soul. Altogether, such emotionally precise language. He *confess* to piano, hold nothing back. Possible to say things beyond words. People ask: what is the secret?' She gestured to the score. 'I told: secret all here. But you must miss not one detail – not one conducting space, not one pulse. That is true mastership.'

At school, Sophia had a new best friend, Jessica. They spent their lunch hours reciting the lyrics of Bon Jovi, while I sat by in silence, calculating how much practice time remained before bed. I had set the clock in motion: the arithmetic that would dominate my life for years to come. Ninety minutes before school meant another eighty minutes before homework, and then seventy after dinner.

'What about this one? *Tommy used to work on the docks …*'

'*Wol-hol! Living on a Pray-er!*'

Sophia had started rowing, and her body had become as svelte as an athlete's; her braces had been removed, revealing film-star teeth. I felt a little betrayed by this onset of beauty, which left me stranded in ungainliness, and wondered miserably if the two of us were 'drifting apart'.

One day Mrs Athersmith summoned me into her office.

'Do you or do you not want to be a prefect?' She was a tall, formidable woman, with a broad Northern English accent.

'Yes, I do.'

'Well I've just had the head of the middle school ask me if Anna Goldsworthy even knows how to speak, because you never make any contribution to prefect meetings.'

Did nobody understand? I was an artist! I had better things to do than speak at prefect meetings.

'You've a good mind, young lady, and the world needs good minds to speak up.'

I nodded to placate her, knowing that words could only take you so far. If only I could play a Chopin étude in prefect meetings: *that* would be a contribution.

'Would you prefer to have your prefecture removed?' she warned me, as she showed me to the door. 'I can do that, you know.'

I caught the bus home tearfully, resolving to make such a sacrifice for Chopin, if necessary, and rushed inside to confess my troubles to the piano. Gradually, the études consoled me. When I snuck into the kitchen for a break, I overheard my mother's worried voice in the living room.

'All she ever does is play the piano. Do you think it's healthy?'

My father muttered something.

'Elsie says Sophia has started going out with boyfriends.'

I snorted to myself, contemptuously. *Boyfriends*. Who needed such trifles? I had the piano as my lover.

❀

Several weeks later, my parents announced that they had bid successfully on the house in Rose Street.

'Hooray!' shouted my sister. 'We're going to be millionaires!'

My brother ran into his bedroom to collect his juggling balls, and I leaned back in my chair, pleased that my masterplan had been successful. 'Does this mean we'll get a grand piano?'

'Only if you can find one you're happy with,' said my father.

That weekend, he took me back to Festival Music, where we were no longer playing make-believe.

'Believe you me, there's been a lot of interest in this piano,' said the salesman, 'but I haven't sold it. Refused to. Far as I was concerned, it already belonged to you.'

Sixty days later, the piano and I were installed in the music room of the new house. The piano was a Yamaha C3, with a polished ebony finish; at six foot one inch, it fitted perfectly into my bay window. Each afternoon when I returned from school, I dropped my bag in my bedroom and entered the small spaceship of this window, practising Chopin études until it was dark. Through the gauze curtains, I watched pedestrians walking up and down the street. Sometimes they stopped to listen, and my practice took on a new intensity. The more I practised, the more I wanted to, as I discovered the rapture of virtuosity, of physical mastery.

After studying the fifth and seventeenth études, I moved on to the first, *traditionally the most difficult*. I applied the magnifying glass of slow practice: checking its joinery, the exact moments of relaxation and regrouping, listening to the interior story of pulse. When I attempted it at full tempo, I was astonished to find that I could play it. Spurred on, I played it faster and faster, intoxicated by speed. I put on a CD of Vladimir Ashkenazy performing at superhuman tempo, and decided to race him. As I rode beside him, the wind beat in our ears and I matched him bar by bar, marvelling at the sight of my hands flickering beneath me at the keyboard, both part of me and yet not part of me.

Afterwards, I attempted the étude without the CD. Away from the slipstream of Ashkenazy's playing, I could no longer play it: there was a sudden tension in my hands that acted as a brake. I had reduced the étude to something mechanical and was duly punished.

'Chopin is epitome of virtuosity, yes,' Mrs Sivan reminded me. 'But *never* sport in music. Each étude greatest piece of music also.'

I had to return to the beginning: to coax myself once more to trust my hands, and my hands to trust the keyboard.

'Exactly,' she said. 'This is true freedom. Not just fish in water. Much freer even! Fish in world! Fish in *universe!* Diving into oceans, flying through skies!'

That year, at the Adelaide Eisteddfod, I received my first first prize. When my father came home from work that evening, he asked how it went.

'I won,' I said, experimentally. I had always wondered how these words might feel in my mouth. They were less substantial than I had hoped.

'About time someone recognised your talent,' he said, and scissor-hopped sideways over the Chesterfield to hug me. That was the joy.

'Of course I am glad,' said Mrs Sivan at my next lesson. 'But never rely on opinion. You're learning if you're winning or if you're losing. In fact, you're learning even more when you're losing. You're learning not to depend. Never go to the clouds, never go to *hell*. Stay on ground. They can put you up, put you down. Doesn't matter.'

'I don't know,' my father said. 'Anna's been working hard, and I think she deserved this.'

'Of course. What I promise: the more you will work, the more you will have. Anna, my darling, it's never easy life. Enormous rewarding? Enormous. We are chosen people? Absolutely. But – this world not appreciate. Not paying for it.'

I nodded enthusiastically, more than ready to be a martyr to my art, especially when awarded first prizes.

'We do spiritual job, and not necessary all spiritual job has right equivalent in material reward. Do not expect that piano will make you millionaire!' She laughed. 'But our life *so* rich.

We getting paid always, by happiness. And by sense of belonging to most important thing in our life.'

At school, I openly told the other students that I planned to be a pianist. In this society of aspiring doctors and lawyers and businessmen, it sounded as reckless as joining the circus, and I enjoyed their shock.

'You might need to be a little more practical,' said a classmate. 'Everyone has dreams, but you also need to think about money.'

'Who needs money?' I scoffed. 'Music is a spiritual job.'

In bed each night, after hours of practice, a synthesis took place in my mind, so that my thoughts seemed to become musical processes. The day's worries melded into polyphony, and then consonance; my anxieties about prefect meetings resolved in a cadence, the sweet *tierce de Picardie* of sleep. When I woke in the morning, I went straight to the piano before my thoughts could reconfigure themselves as words. My practice was still sometimes distracted, as I searched for openings into that parallel world of hearing. But I found that I understood more and more of what Mrs Sivan said in her lessons, and that I could remember it at home, at least for a time.

'You will go deeper and deeper every year,' Mrs Sivan promised me. 'Music is a magic door opening inside you.'

Opening that magic door became the central purpose of my life, self-improvement at the piano my only narrative. I came to fear the moment of my death as a moment of reckoning, in which the practice would have to stop. But for now, such a moment seemed infinitely far off. At the end of that year, I once more sat my Eighth Grade exam. This time, I received an A-plus, and the Thelma Dent Memorial Scholarship for the top mark in the state. The dark days of the C were in the past; my hair was growing; my hands quickening into life. Sitting at my piano in my bay window I soared towards my future: a fish in the universe, swimming past stars.

Chapter 9. Liszt

As I practised, my mother moved through the rooms of our new house, stripping and polishing the floorboards and meticulously repainting the cornices in cream and off-white. My father, installed in his new study, worked hard on his piano book. The printer crunched out draft after draft, much more rapidly than it had with Claude. Each Sunday lunch there was a growing excitement within the family as he read aloud the latest fax from his editor.

In this final scene, I believe Paul should put on a record of Keller playing. This seems to me the only suitable climax for this great work – appropriately cathartic, deeply moving … And I had an idea for a title: Maestro.

In the early drafts of this book, there was much that I recognised, and it was like looking at my own life in a mirror. There were my grandparents, twenty years younger; my first piano lessons with Mrs Sivan; the library stacks where my father and I had researched the Leschetizky school. But with each revision, the mirror became more opaque, until I realised it was no longer my story at all, but a work of fiction. My grandparents swapped hair colours; the library stacks at Dewey Decimal 786.2 were desecrated with a sex scene; and Mrs Sivan became unrecognisable, her outlines overdrawn with those of a different pianist: an alcoholic Austrian, Eduard Keller, living in Darwin.

There was one element of the book that made me uneasy. At the end of the book, Keller dies, closing a final door for his student Paul.

While Keller had lived – no matter how many years since our last consultation – he had been a safety net, offering a faint last hope, a genetic lifeline back to Liszt, Czerny, Leschetizky; there had always been the possibility of returning to his room at the Swan, and preparing myself for a last assault on the world of music. Now I was faced with myself for the first time.

Mrs Sivan was also my lifeline; at times, the degree of my dependency on her troubled me. Sometimes it seemed that I needed her to show me how to play every note; otherwise I floundered through a world I did not understand.

'Not,' she said, when I hinted at my concerns. 'I give seeds and seeds and seeds. You digest, and this knowledge becomes you. Every year growing, every year more doors opening.'

I tried to believe her. Surely, after years of bathing in her radiance, I would inherit her mastery: my hands would become as quick and natural as hers, my understanding as immediate, my emotional freedom as absolute. And yet the more I learned, the more clearly I could hear the gap between her artistry and my schoolgirl sounds.

In this sense Keller was bad for me, the worse possible teacher: revealing perfection to me, and at the same time snatching it away.

Teaching a self-criticism that would never allow me to forget my limits.

The fear of artistic inadequacy occupied my own midnight thoughts, too; it seemed a greater horror than mortality. But come morning, when I sat down at the piano, I was able to set these anxieties aside and believe once more in the endless possibility of improvement. My potential was as yet unmeasured, and therefore infinite. And Mrs Sivan would surely always be around to guide me.

❖

One Tuesday, my father brought a manuscript of *Maestro* to a lesson for Mrs Sivan to read.

'Very interesting book really,' she said the following week. 'Though of course strange to make great pianist *alcoholic*.'

The book was launched in September, at the Adelaide Zoo. There was a light spring rain in the air, and the party crammed into the rotunda, where my brother and I provided background music on piano and clarinet. We might as well have been miming, as our sound was absorbed by those damp, excited bodies, and obliterated by the clink of champagne flutes.

My father made a speech, thanking his editor, agent and various friends, and then read out the dedication to his book: *To four pianists: my parents Jan and Reuben, my daughter Anna, and the finest teacher I have known, Eleonora Sivan.*

Mrs Sivan bowed her head, accepting his acknowledgment; my mother, statuesque in her best clothes, applauded proudly. Somewhere a lion roared, like a distant catastrophe.

Afterwards, as he signed books, I pushed through the

queue: 'Excuse me, but I have the pianist Kate Stevens with me.'

My great-grandmother was already at the front, her large blue eyes watery and aggrieved, demanding to know why he had not thanked my mother.

'Dad, Kate can't stay,' I interrupted her.

He turned to me in relief. 'What's that, Pie?'

'She has a recital tomorrow at Edmund Wright House.'

'Well, good luck! No – whoops! – what am I supposed to say? Break a finger!'

'It's for the Australian Society of Keyboard Music (Adelaide Chapter) Incorporated,' I continued, but he was already signing somebody else's book.

I walked Kate out to the gate, holding her umbrella.

'You should think about joining the society,' she suggested.

'What, the Australian Society of Keyboard Music?' I asked, incredulously. 'But I'm only fifteen.'

'They'll start you off with home recitals. Then if they like you, they'll offer you a Wednesday lunch-hour recital at Edmund Wright House.'

Edmund Wright House was a grand, historic building on King William Street, housing the Office of Births, Deaths and Marriages and a performance space for even more significant events: debut recitals.

'I'll speak to Miss Hopgood about it, and we'll get you started,' she offered.

'Thank you,' I said and returned her umbrella. I stood there at that gate in the rain, dazed by my good fortune, watching her hurry to her car. Then I turned and sprinted through the zoo, past the chattering of the monkeys, back to the party-goers in their delirious cage. The smell of manure and fecundity seeped upwards into the air, pushing me onward like a cloud, and I burst back into the rotunda, damp and exhilarated, ready for our glorious futures, my father's and mine.

At my next piano lesson, I told Mrs Sivan that I had been invited to perform at a home recital. 'It's for the Australian Society of Keyboard Music,' I explained.

'Of course,' she said. 'Kate told. Definitely they must also give you lunch-hour recital. Quality I can guarantee. And excellent that Kate is looking after you. This makes me very proud. Spirit of generosity is *crucial* for music. Some people think knowledge is theirs, to keep, and will not share, but this will kill sounds *immediately*. Music is arts of life, and arts of giving.'

'What shall I play?' I asked.

'In large sense, generosity not just about acts, is way of thinking. The more you have, the more you give. In some ways, it comes together with religious beliefs, of bringing and giving. Always remember: only what you give is yours.'

'Should I learn some Liszt?' I suggested.

'For home recital, we can decide. But for lunch recital, must be very special program. Bach, Mozart, Chopin études, yes, but must be something more … Of course!' Her eyes lit up. 'Liszt *Rigoletto* paraphrase! You will do beautifully. Absolute freedom and fantasy. Tells story of Verdi's opera, and brings it to life in piano.'

She disappeared into her music library, returning with the score.

'We talk about generosity. Liszt *completely* generous musician, and completely open. I admire this man more and more. Very interesting how enormously educated he was. Czerny was his teacher, which meant he had Beethoven roots, straightaway. But also, he learns from everything and everybody. Happy to give, and happy to take! Sometimes takes from Chopin, by the way, who not always so generous – except to piano, who he loves.'

I moved Chopin to one side in my mind, making room for Liszt.

'Liszt understands that poetry, literature, opera, ballet, all coming from the piano and to the piano. The richer you are, like a person, in knowledge and imagination, the more what?'

'The more you can give?' I guessed.

'Exactly. Because the more you have in your store.'

She put the music on the stand and turned to the first page; I thrilled to the sight of the left-hand octaves.

'Liszt *very* philosophical composer, and busy always with three questions: love, life and death. What is it negative and what is positive? How much wrong do we have in our right? It depends on situation and place.'

'Of course,' I said, imagining myself playing these octaves in a home recital.

'Devil and God. Kindness, generosity and nastiness: always was subject for a lot of musicians. The same as in literature, only in sounds.'

I reached for the keyboard, but she caught my hand without pausing. 'Here we have opera, full story, with real characters. Rigoletto is basically clown – how do you say – *jester*, and

tragic figure really. And his daughter Gilda, completely innocent. And then we have the Duke, *professional* at seduction.
We begin with philosophical introduction, from Liszt, not
from Verdi.'

I tried the opening octaves, and discovered that they were
more difficult than they looked.

'Not! Never just octaves for octaves' sake! People always
ask: what is secret of octaves? I tell them: no secret! Octaves
just music! First we ask: what is structure of this phrase?' She
took my thumb in her hand, sketching the outline of the first
phrase. 'B goes on walk up to F sharp, yes? Then E-major
second inversion, like question.'

Now that I could see its skeleton, the first phrase was easy;
I repeated it for her, with my thumb alone.

'Always phrases, always words, never empty notes. But
within each word: *exact* spelling.'

I tried the phrase now in octaves, which dropped easily
from my wrist.

'Exactly! And now they will tell you that you have *natural
octaves*.' She laughed. 'As if born with them, as little baby.'

I continued through the opening pages.

'Not. You playing here. Liszt *absolutely* free at piano. Greatest compliment is it looks easy, not difficult. At same time, he
is always – how do you say? Busy by his hands.'

'Fidgeting?'

'Yes exactly. So excited by piano. Difficult for Liszt to play
simple phrase, without embellishment. Very hyperactive man
in some ways. But so easy: just positions, just *handing down* the
piano.'

She showed me each position in a block chord. I imitated

her, and then when I played the passage as written, it cascaded down the piano with an improvisatory freedom.

'Exactly! More fantasy and less logical discipline leads to madhouse. But logical discipline not enough. Discipline without fantasy leads to what?'

'Post-mortem examination?'

'Exactly.'

At home, for hour after hour, I addressed myself to the *Rigoletto* paraphrase. A fortnight later, I offered to perform it for my grandfather, as a dress rehearsal for the home recital.

'That would be a great pleasure,' he said. 'I have some pieces I would like to play for you also, on pipe organ and piano.'

Since his retirement, my grandfather had taken lessons in both instruments, and was making rapid progress. My grandmother, of legendary sight-reading status in the family, had surrendered the piano to him entirely, and he practised six hours a day. I felt alternately proud of and exasperated by his achievements, as he stalked me through the AMEB exams. Later that year, we would both be sitting for our Associate Diplomas, which seemed somehow against the natural order of things.

'The two of us can enjoy an afternoon of convivial music-making,' he continued. 'I believe your holidays begin next week, so might I nominate Tuesday as an appropriate occasion?'

The following Tuesday, he picked me up from home and took me to Pilgrim church in the city. At the organ console, he rolled up his sleeves and sat down, adjusting the stops like a pilot settling into his cockpit, and then launched into the toccata from Boëllmann's *Suite Gothique*. There was a great backward thrust of sound; standing beside him, I understood the megalomanic thrill of playing the organ. I marvelled at his virtuosity and his co-ordination, his hands moving between manuals and snatching at stops, his feet on the pedal-board agile as a tap dancer.

'As you may have observed, this robust toccata closely resembles in style Widor's famous toccata, the last movement from his Organ Symphony No. 5. But neither toccata should be confused with the toccatas of Johann Sebastian Bach,' he said, and demonstrated Bach's Toccata in D Minor. 'Which themselves differ markedly from the fantasias, and which are another genre entirely to the preludes and fugues.'

Many fugues later, I retreated to a pew, where I took the score of *Rigoletto* out of my satchel. I tried to read it in the dusky light, practising my octaves in the vibrating air, and then dozed off, encased by decibels. When I woke up, my grandfather was still playing; some time later, he emerged from the console, sprightly and enlivened, and we returned to my grandparents' house for dinner.

'Three hours does seem a very long concert, dear,' my grandmother said gently, as she served the potatoes.

'Bear in mind that you are speaking to two great apprecia-tors of music,' my grandfather responded. 'At any rate, that was only the entrée. Our next course comprises a range of delicacies from the piano repertoire.'

After dinner, as I performed *Rigoletto*, the raucous gran-deur of an organ still clanged in my ears, and my octave pas-sages were not as thrilling as I had anticipated.

'Very fine work, darling,' he said, grinning proudly. 'Your progress under Mrs Sivan does not surprise me, given my initial impressions of her. However, I might also add that it is harder to play the slower pieces well. Allow me to offer some empirical proof.'

He sat down at the piano and performed the Chopin Waltz in A Minor.

'Yes I know,' I said, 'but—'

He launched into the C-sharp Minor Waltz before I could defend myself, expanded on his argument with two Mendelssohn *Songs without Words*, and concluded with the Chopin Nocturne in E-flat Major.

'I hope you will agree that I have made my point,' he said, and gently placed the red felt cover over the keyboard, tucking it up for the night, and closed the lid.

The following weekend, I stood outside the front door of Miss Hopgood's house in Brighton, feeling anxious about *Rigoletto*. It was not yet two hundred per cent secure, and I suspected it was too early to be playing it in public, but it seemed the only piece worthy of such a grand occasion. My father rang the bell and Miss Hopgood came to the door.

'You must be Anna, and you must be the proud father, Mr Goldsworthy?'

'Peter,' said my father, reaching out his hand.

Miss Hopgood was a grandmotherly figure in pale-blue cashmere, with her hair bundled up in a topknot, snowy-white as lamb's wool. 'Come through, come through.' She led us into a room dominated by a grand piano on one side, and a large table on the other, supporting an afternoon tea of butterfly cakes, pikelets and egg sandwiches. A small audience perched in the middle, on three rows of dining-room chairs;

a young soldier in uniform watched gravely from a photo on the sideboard.

'I must introduce you to our vice-president,' Miss Hopgood said, leading us to an elderly man in a white cap. 'Captain Frizzel, this is Anna, and her very proud father, Mr Goldsworthy.'

'Peter,' my father repeated.

Captain Frizzel unfolded from his seat, looming over both of us. 'How do you do. Welcome to the society.'

Kate began the recital with an electrifying performance of the first Chopin scherzo. At the half-diminished chord that announces the reprise, the middle-aged woman in front of me jerked awake in her seat, and the afternoon tea vibrated in alarm. After some polite applause, an elderly society member stepped up to the piano and sight-read his way through a Schubert impromptu, blushing wildly behind his moustache.

There was a hum of appreciation throughout the room: 'You do have such a lovely touch, Arthur.'

To close, I played the *Rigoletto* paraphrase. It lacked freedom and fantasy, and I was glad that neither Mrs Sivan nor my grandfather was there to hear it. But my father winked at me afterwards, and I felt I could hold my head up through afternoon tea.

'Very nice,' said Miss Hopgood, offering around the sandwiches. 'Wouldn't it be lovely, Captain Frizzel, to feature both of these young ladies at next year's September lunch-hour series?'

'A fine idea,' he said gallantly. He fixed his pale blue eyes on me. 'A very challenging piece, that *Rigoletto* paraphrase.'

'I don't know why people bother with paraphrases,' Arthur said. 'As if there was not enough piano repertoire around.'

'Paraphrases might just be coming back into fashion,' Miss Hopgood suggested. 'Didn't that Russian pianist play *Rigoletto* in the last Sydney International Competition? What was his name – Tarasov?'

'Now *that* was a wonderful performance!' said a woman in a beret. 'I never would have recognised it as the same piece.'

'Indeed he did,' said Arthur, through a mouthful of curried egg. 'And as I think I said at the time: if someone could combine Tarasov's technique with my musicality – why, that would be the perfect pianist!'

My grandfather accompanied me to my next lesson with Mrs Sivan and offered to play her a Chopin waltz. She listened respectfully, making only a couple of suggestions; as I traded places with him on the stool, I hoped she would be equally gentle with me. But she stopped me when I came to the second page of the *Rigoletto* paraphrase.

'Duke must be seductive! Other way we have no problem!' She laughed. 'No story – everybody can go home! I know is difficult: you are fifteen-year-old girl. More Gilda than Duke, really. But to tell this story you must be everything: Gilda *and* Rigoletto *and* Maddalena *and* conductor *and* orchestra *and* Duke *and* director *and* a million other things!'

'I have told Anna that it's more difficult to play the simple things well,' my grandfather interrupted.

'Liszt always *very* interested in seduction,' Mrs Sivan continued. 'He believes you can seduce near everyone.'

'I'm not sure that I can endorse that view,' my grandfather said.

'Of course. But depends on how talented the seducer. Because everyone has their weakness. For example, you're strong against the winds, you're strong against compliments, you can be strong against money – that's a lot of people.'

My grandfather nodded.

'Then somebody will tell you how fantastic your grandchildren are, and immediately you surrender!'

My grandfather laughed. 'But you have to admit, she's not so bad, my granddaughter, is she?'

'Not at all! I love this girl!' She hugged me. 'Basically, we cannot guarantee immunity from seduction. Without our knowledge we can be under spell, and this *always* fascinates Liszt. If Mephistopheles put his real face on everything, of course we know to avoid him; but when he is charming man, who says beautiful things, then you have no idea. Here, we start with left hand – like serenade.' She plucked at the accompaniment, which floated through the air like a guitar. 'And now we choose our tenor. You like Pavarotti?' She performed the melody for me as Pavarotti, each sound swollen with emotion. 'Or perhaps you prefer Placido Domingo?' She played it again, this time with more suavity, and laughed. 'Possibilities *endless*! Liszt understands seduction very well. Absolutely everybody was in love with him.' She dropped her voice. 'Excuse me for saying, but you are big girl now: Liszt was a womaniser – natural. But more than this. He was *seducer* of audiences. In this way, he was opposite to Chopin, who hated big stage. Liszt was inspired by Paganini on violin, by enormous possibilities of virtuosity, to excite, to thrill!

People go crazy, women faint. Sometimes it seems beyond human: even like devil power. Liszt's pianism is a sort of *magic arts*.'

＊

At the beginning of the next year, a new violinist arrived at our school from Singapore, Yoong-Han Chan. He was shy and quiet in class, but when he performed a Paganini caprice, he did seem possessed by a devil power. As he played, he sniffed as loudly as a bulldog, rolling his eyes into the back of his skull so that the whites blazed terrifyingly at the audience. Each sound he made slashed through the music room, pinning me to my seat; by comparison, I felt like a hobbyist, a genteel lady pianist.

'What do you plan to do when you finish school?' our new headmaster asked in my student interview. 'Your academic results are excellent.'

'I'm going to be a musician!' I declared.

He focussed on me momentarily, and then returned his attention to the courtyard outside the window.

'That's all very well, but look at Yoong-Han Chan. That's a musician. You wouldn't even think twice about it. But the same can't really be said about you and me.'

I felt a righteous anger, and resolved once again to show *them*. That year, I won most of the sections I entered at the Adelaide Eisteddfod, and was awarded the Yamaha Medallion for most promising pianist under sixteen. Miss Hopgood called to confirm my September recital in Edmund Wright House, and my father designed a flyer on his Macintosh:

Piano Recital
26 September, 12.10–12.50
Anna Goldsworthy
Winner of the 1990 Adelaide Eisteddfod Yamaha Medallion
for Most Promising Pianist under Sixteen

'You can't write that!' I exclaimed. 'That's showing off.'

'Listen to me, Pie.' He spun around in his chair and addressed me seriously. 'I always thought the world would beat a path to my door, but sometimes it needs a bit of encouragement. The sooner you understand that, the better.'

He photocopied the flyers onto fluorescent yellow paper at the newsagent, and gave me a stack to take to school. I hid them all in my locker, except for one, which I pinned up on an obscure noticeboard in a distant corridor, hoping desperately that my headmaster and classmates might find their way over there and read it.

On the morning of 26 September, my father took me to Edmund Wright House to rehearse. It was a dazzling space when empty, with its gilt ceiling and ancient, diffused light. As I played on the Steinway, I felt as free as a child in a bouncing castle, sending my sound around the walls and up to the ceiling, tracing out its ornate grooves, and then back to my father in the audience.

'How's the acoustic?' I called out.

'Don't overdo it, Pie. Save some energy for the concert.'

But the concert was nearly three hours away, which was more than ten thousand seconds, and might have been forever. I continued performing, enraptured by the sound of

Liszt glittering in the air, until the piano-tuner arrived and it was time to go home and rest.

When we returned at lunchtime, I felt less confident. My father parked the car several blocks away, and as we walked I avoided the cracks between the paving stones, unable to speak. My new chiffon concert dress had seemed to have transformative powers when my mother bought it for me but now, as the spring breeze pressed it against my breasts and between my legs, it felt flimsy, as if I were approaching the stage naked.

My father whistled the theme from *Rigoletto*. He seemed happy and excited in a way that was distinctly unsympathetic, and I glared at him.

'What's wrong, Pie?'

'Can you please cut that out?'

He walked in silence for a moment, and then started whistling again. I was struck by my aloneness, by the gulf that separated us. My father might be on my side, but what did that mean, finally, when I was the one up onstage, and he was in the audience far away?

'What if I have a memory lapse?' I gasped.

My father shrugged. 'So what if you do? It won't kill you.'

How could he be so casual?

'In fact, you probably *will* have a memory lapse,' he continued. 'Big deal! If I know you, you'll improvise your way out of it, and hardly anyone will notice. Everyone will be wishing you well, anyway.'

We turned into King William Street, where there was a line of people spilling out of Edmund Wright House, waiting for tickets. I veered away, as if stabbed.

'Wonderful turn-out!' my father exclaimed. I hid behind his back as he waved to his friends, and then scrambled through a side door, where I bumped into Miss Hopgood.

'There you are!' She looked flushed. 'What a crowd! We had to refresh the float. Just come through here to the dressing room, and I'll be back to get you in ten minutes.'

Ten minutes was still six hundred seconds, I reassured myself, as the air pressed in around me in the dressing room. A lot could happen in six hundred seconds. I took the music out of my satchel, leaving it in a safe pile by the door for emergency reference. *Five hundred and forty seconds*. I double-checked that I was wearing my good-luck bra, and reapplied my lipstick. *Two hundred and forty seconds*. 'You are going to seduce that audience,' I said to the frightened face in the mirror, but it did not look convinced.

Miss Hopgood knocked on the door. 'It's time,' she beamed, pinkly.

Of course it was time. I walked out to the stage, my new shoes clunking loudly on the floor. *Don't trip, don't trip*. This familiar mantra carried me to the front, where I smiled and bowed at the far wall, as though it were a distant friend, ignoring the intrusion of the audience between us. As I sat down at the piano, my right leg trembled in furious vibrato; I pretended it did not belong to me. If I concentrated on looking calm, I might yet become it.

'True artist must be comfortable from beginning,' Mrs Sivan had told me, 'onstage is not time for *warm up*,' but the Bach and Mozart passed for me as if in a trance, apart from a momentary stumble in the fugue, from which I recovered immediately, as my father had promised. Once more I was standing and bowing to the audience, but I felt better able to look at it now, having survived this far. There was my entire extended family, scaling upwards from smallest cousins to grandparents. The sun's rays sliced through the room like a child's drawing, illuminating my grandmother at the far left, dabbing her eyes with a handkerchief; and my mother sitting beside her, clutching her blouse. Behind them was Mrs Sivan with her husband Isaac; over there, towards the back, Sophia and Jessica and Captain Frizzel. Sitting obediently in their seats, the audience seemed friendly and containable, no longer the latent lynch mob of the street.

I sat back down to begin the Liszt, becoming aware of the grainy texture of the keyboard beneath my fingers, its mellow, well-worn sound. My thighs relaxed, which I experienced as a type of quickening, a sign that the recital had come to life. As I eased into the Duke's serenade, I was at once the seducer and the seduced. *Perhaps this is going well*, a voice said in my head, but I released it into the air and continued with my magic arts.

Afterwards, I submitted to the violence of the applause and Miss Hopgood brought me a large bouquet of flowers – roses, lilies of the valley, irises. I placed them on the side of the piano as I played an encore, and then returned to the stage for the curtain calls.

When the applause came to an end, I waited in the foyer, catching my breath. My grandfather came out first, tearful and mute. 'Just beautiful, dear,' he said finally, as he grasped my hand.

Mrs Sivan embraced me warmly. 'Lots of excellent things, my darling. In some ways you surprise even me. You prove to me that you can be concert pianist.'

'Good one, kiddo!' said my father, as he danced out. 'Looked like you'd been doing this forever.'

'Who sent those gorgeous flowers?' my mother asked, scrutinising the card: *Hope it goes well*. 'Everyone we know is here. It must have been my secretary! Wasn't that lovely of her? And *quite* unnecessary!'

I knew immediately who had sent them: a beautiful boy in my French class, Sam, who I often glanced at just to see if he was looking. He had discovered my flyer in its distant corridor, and apologised that he would be interstate. Back at school, I would be too embarrassed to acknowledge the gift.

'This girl taught me great lesson,' Mrs Sivan continued. 'As a child, she was a little ... aloof. I didn't understand: didn't recognise. Kate I could see immediately. So emotional, so excited! But Anna – always holding a little back. Always think first, and after feel. But now, full revolution from inside! How her eyes have changed! Beautiful eyes – yes? So warm!'

'Oh, so you're the teacher, are you?' asked an elderly lady. 'What, she *still* has lessons? Shouldn't she be the one doing the teaching?'

We returned to the hall for Kate's recital, but my heart thumped so loudly in my chest that I scarcely heard a note. I wanted to be up there again on the stage, my hands warm and nimble on the keyboard beneath me, the fragrance of the flowers wafting into the air, blending with the music. I would perform encore after encore after encore; people would go crazy and women faint; I would seduce them all with my magic arts; I had discovered that playing a recital was the best way of being alive.

Chapter 10. Prokofiev

MY DEBUT RECITAL had dominated the horizon entirely, obscuring any future beyond it. Now that it was over, I was faced with my final school exams, less than a year away. Clearly, I had to win the Don Maynard Prize for the state's top music student, to continue Kate Stevens' tradition and deliver the huge shock that Mrs Sivan had prophesied.

'Is not enough to make same shock as Kate,' she told me. 'Must be *new* shock entirely. You will play Chopin ballade, and tell great story of heroism. Will be *absolutely* mature. But also, must be something else.'

'Liszt?' I asked.

'Not. We need something completely contrasted … must be Prokofiev!'

She disappeared into her library and returned with the Prokofiev Toccata, which she placed on the music stand.

'Please tell me: who is Prokofiev?' she asked.

'A Russian composer born in 1891.'

'Of course. But who is Prokofiev man, not facts?'

I hesitated, and she opened the score.

'Very important to understand every composer like a live person, who intentionally or unintentionally reflects on their own experiences. Exactly like writer. No one writer is writing about what they do not know.' She spun around to my father. 'What you think: *Maestro* work of fiction?'

He shrugged. 'Essentially. Which isn't to say it's not inspired by life.'

'Exactly! The more they say it's fictional, the more it's exactly real! And music even more honest than literature. Why? Because music basically abstract, which gives enormous freedom for composer to be completely truthful. This *very* important to understand.'

She scrutinised the score, like a palm reader.

'All answers here. All character, all autobiography. For example, this is very young man, in love with his own powers. *Definitely* wants to make huge impression!' She demonstrated the repeated notes of the opening with a funky, insolent ease. 'We have new style entirely: rhythm *hugely* important, and garmonic revolution. Of course there are dissonances. What you expect? Prokofiev is modern composer, emancipated in spirit, reflecting the world around him. And what you think, world not completely changed?'

'Of course.'

'Absolutely! This is mechanistic age. Century of enormous destruction. And destruction a *million* times more easy than building up.'

'You can't make an omelette without breaking eggs,' I quoted. We had been studying the Russian revolution at school.

She smiled, grimly. 'In some ways, Prokofiev very trustful. First he left Russia, and then he returned.'

'Why?'

She shrugged. 'They wanted Stravinsky back too, but Stravinsky much more careful. *We love you, and your music very popular in our country.* Very good, said Stravinsky, love me from over there. I will send you more of my work.' She chuckled, darkly. 'But Prokofiev was maybe more nostalgic, and did believe to these words. And then what? *Do what I say, or we will find another Prokofiev.* Devastating for this man, of course.' There was a sudden weariness in her face. 'Then died on same day as Stalin.'

'Do you remember it?'

She gazed out of the window at the tree with the yellow leaves. It was her favourite tree, she had told me, because of its optimism. 'Everyone grieving for Stalin, no-one for Prokofiev. I was child, and *very* upset that we had lost our beloved leader. I wrote great memorial poem, full of emotion and tragedy.'

She turned back to the piano and relief flooded her face. 'Always remember Prokofiev *greatest* master of the piano. He is from our school, by the way – learned from Annette Essipoff. Completely revolutionary, but with this *enormous* level of pianism and culture. And when you're working with this foundation of knowledge, what do you feel?'

'Confident?'

'Exactly. Security. Because you know that the answers already here. Different from Stravinsky in this way, who doesn't care about pianist. In Prokofiev, you don't need to invent your pianistic solutions. You need only to find.'

She began the opening once more.

'First of all, conduct. And always remember *pulse*: pulse of your hearing, pulse of your inside, pulse of your feeling, and not pulse of destruction. Basically, you are playing percussion instrument inside piano.'

She dropped her voice to a whisper, tapping my arm: 'And a *one* da and a *two* da and a *one* da *ding! Da*-da-*da*-da-*da*-da-*da*-da-*da*-da-and-a-*two*-ding!'

She conveyed this rhythm to me like an electric charge, until I caught it, in each jiggling cell of my body.

'Words important, yes? But punctuation *vitally* important to meaning of words. We must know exact grammar of every pulse. Remember always: *emotional perspective of punctuation*.'

'Emotional perspective of punctuation,' I repeated, uncertainly.

'Exactly! Very nice expression, which – by the way – I just invented.' She laughed. 'Please remember, because I will forget myself, and have to invent again.'

Perspective of any sort – emotional or otherwise – eluded me at that time. Besides winning the Don Maynard Prize, there were a number of other goals I had to achieve. My English teacher, Mr Clarke, had indicated that he expected me to do 'very well' in the final exam, with a significant, terrifying wink. I knew what he meant: the Tennyson Medal for the top English student in the state, the most coveted of the matriculation prizes, which my uncle Jeff had secured for the family twenty years earlier. At the same time, I had to secure my position as dux of the school, achieve perfect scores in double mathematics, guide the school debating team to victory in the state finals, maintain my domination of the Adelaide Eisteddfod, and prepare two recitals for the Australian Society of Keyboard Music. I was also about to tour Europe with the school choir, performing piano solos, culminating in a concert at St John's, Smith Square, London. It was my first trip overseas: it would have to be a triumphant international debut.

I knew I was being greedy with my demands, and weighed up their relative importance in my head, wondering which I could sacrifice to secure the others. But none was negotiable. Achievement had become my way of knowing myself: I no longer even experienced it as a pleasure, only as the relief of non-failure. Perhaps the universe would consider some other Faustian bargain: lifelong spinsterhood, for example, or the divorce of my parents?

'All musicians superstitious, doesn't matter what they say,' Mrs Sivan had told me. 'Like any profession with large pressure. Find me surgeon who is not superstitious! Of course, superstition is experience of centuries, and could be wrong, could be right. Could be wrong because they didn't know, or could be right because it's coming from experience. But onstage especially, is enough to have only *little* doubt to cause problems.'

Over the years of my piano lessons, I had inherited a set of Russian superstitions to complement my home-grown ones. I lurched away from friends who attempted to kiss me under thresholds; I filled tea cups to the brim, so that they sloshed into the saucer, guaranteeing the tea-drinker a full life. My personal cosmology was becoming increasingly elaborate, combining prime-number worship with Russian lore, but there was too much at stake in my life: I could not afford a little doubt.

On the plane to Europe, as my fellow choristers leafed through the *Vogue* Christmas special, I recited the Fibonacci sequence to myself in frantic prayer, fingering each number in my mind like a rosary bead, to guarantee us a safe landing. Later, as we wandered through the streets of Europe, the Prokofiev Toccata played constantly in my head, its *moto perpetuo* a soundtrack to my anxiety. Everything I saw was pattern and rhythm, as if my life were a giant toccata, expanding on the smallest of motivic cells. In Stockholm, the incorrect choice of cobblestone could cause a memory lapse; in Lübeck, the sloppy placement of a postage stamp would imperil my family at home, unsupervised.

'What on earth is this?' my cousin asked one afternoon, as she sorted through our laundry. We were billeted together in Husum, a small town in northern Germany. She was holding up the vestiges of my good-luck bra, which through repeated washings had become tissue-thin as an elf garment. It had lost all elasticity, so that I had to secure it with a series of safety pins; even with these, it offered no support other than magic.

'None of your business.' As I snatched it back from her, it fell apart in my hands, and I began to cry.

'It's okay to feel homesick,' she said gently. 'I do too.'

That night, I dreamt I performed the Prokofiev Toccata in the Adelaide Town Hall. The piano was strangely unresponsive, and I realised, midway through the performance, that it was not a piano at all, but an electric keyboard. As I played, its compass contracted to four octaves, then two, and then one. I tried to recompose the toccata to fit, but could not make it work, continually beaching myself on its sides. The vast audience muttered and jeered, and then abandoned me, while I floundered onstage for hours, trapped within an octave.

The sour taste of failure was still with me at rehearsal the following morning, when our choir director made an announcement.

'Girls, I want you to listen very carefully. The mayor has invited us to give a concert tonight in the Husum Town Hall. This is a *very special* honour.' He paused significantly; the senior choristers made appropriate noises of surprise and delight. 'I regret to say they only have an electric keyboard, but I am still going to ask Anna to perform the Prokofiev Toccata.'

'Unbelievable,' I muttered, shaking my head.

His eyebrows shot down his forehead. 'If Anna thinks this is beneath her artistic standards, then I suggest she say so immediately.'

I contemplated this. It would not be unreasonable to refuse: an electric keyboard could scarcely do justice to the Prokofiev Toccata. But perhaps this was cowardice speaking, rather than artistic integrity.

Abruptly, I realised I had had enough. My good-luck bra had abandoned me, and now *this*. I would no longer be bullied by secret messages; it was time to confront my fears.

'I'm happy to do it.'

His eyebrows relaxed upwards. 'That's what I call *being a trouper*, and that's what being in this choir is all about.'

That night, I wore a normal bra to the concert, and ignored the secret messages of cobblestones as we walked to the town hall. *Be normal*, I reminded myself, as my mind veered towards the Fibonacci. As we sang our first bracket of carols, a group of local boys leaned over the mezzanine, pointing out the good-looking girls; around me, my fellow choristers flicked their shiny hair.

At the end of the first set, I stepped out to take on the electric keyboard and all it represented. The keyboard was unresponsive, and deaf to nuance, but I thought of it as a percussion instrument, and danced my Prokofiev on it as an exorcism, a plea for sanity. It felt lonely out there without the Fibonacci sequence looking after me, but I willed my hands to behave, and for the most part they did. As I approached the final *glissando*, a voice in my head dared me to end on a wrong note to save my family from natural disaster. I ignored it and played the right notes, trusting that the ripples of this octave D would neither travel so far, nor be so malignant.

It was an average performance on an unresponsive instrument, but as I jumped from my seat to take a bow it felt like a great life triumph. I had remained on that stage for four minutes instead of hours; the audience had not haemorrhaged; the keyboard had maintained its generous compass of seven and a quarter octaves. Perhaps now I could join the world of normal mortals, unperturbed by magic, and flick my hair at the good-looking boys.

❅

Back home in Adelaide, as a recovering magical thinker, I had to find new ways to secure my goals. I devised a schedule, enlisting every available moment to the purpose of self-improvement. Each morning I woke at a quarter to six, recorded *Aerobics Oz Style* off the television, and practised for an hour before breakfast. At school, I completed as much homework as possible in lessons, returning home to practise all evening, with breaks only for an aerobics work-out, dinner and the completion of any remaining homework. I was in bed by 9.30, with twenty minutes' designated reading time, ready to resume my training regime the following morning.

'Be careful not to burn yourself out, Pie,' my father said one night, as my family watched *The Comedy Company*.

I ignored him and returned to the music room for Prokofiev training. In the distance, I could hear them laughing. Why was I the only one, in this family of sloths, intent on bettering myself, on purifying myself through work? I slammed the door and practised more loudly. Who had time for comedy, anyway? I set the metronome at fifty per cent, and then again at seventy-five per cent; I practised the left-hand part alone, until I knew it by memory.

'Not!' said Mrs Sivan the following week, when I demonstrated the results of my training. 'Where is humour?'

'Humour?'

'Of course! Prokofiev has *greatest* sense of humour, in *millions* of varieties. Humoristic, sarcastic, sometimes even sardonic.'

I started again, trying to be humorous.

'Not. Joke *enormous* here. For example, what do we have here?' She dropped her voice: *'Did I tell you? – did I tell you? – did I tell you, yes?* Gossip, gossip and gossip, coming around you, in polyphony. And suddenly, trombones.'

She played the left hand, and a trombone section materialised in the room, sounding out the theme in augmentation, until she laughed, delighted. 'Full discipline, of course, but at same time, full imagination. Prokofiev *absolutely* extroverted in this piece. He is young man, in love with his powers! You must never be just athlete, or schoolgirl. Must be artist, please, and only.'

As my schoolgirl years drew to a close, I had to make plans for the future. At school, the vice-principal urged me to study pure mathematics; my mother spoke hypothetically of law, as a sensible back-up plan; my father suggested a combined degree, of arts and music.

'Do you think Anna should consider study overseas?' my father asked Mrs Sivan.

She considered this. 'I will give everything I can, and forever. But what I can't give? Surroundings.' Outside the window, a car backed out of the driveway opposite. Its headlights flicked through the darkening room, and then disappeared. 'When I remember what we had in Russia: Kirov opera and ballet, every weekend, and *huge* and biggest personalities all around: Shostakovich, Khachaturian, Kabalevsky, Rostropovich, Richter, Gilels, Oistrakh ...' She counted their names on her fingers, laughing at the excess. 'I not say Russia is perfect, not. But in certain backgrounds, when you have material deprivation, immediately you come to spiritual.'

'Do you think Anna should go to Russia?' my father asked.

'In current situation, impossible. Safety I cannot guarantee. But what I can guarantee? That she will be learning always, like sponge, and forever. Please, once more Prokofiev.'

That winter, the pianist Douglas Owen returned to Adelaide, to give a subscription recital for the Australian Society of Keyboard Music at Elder Hall. He was four years older than me, and a gentle soul, well-mannered and chivalrous; my father and I had met him briefly on his previous visit to

Adelaide, when he was still a law student in Melbourne. Soon afterwards, he had won a competition in Italy, and moved to New York to study at the Juilliard School.

Douglas's recital was a large event in Adelaide's musical calendar, and as my father and I pushed through the bustling foyer, I felt the reflected glory of our famous acquaintance.

'What was it that Douglas used to say about studying law?' I asked, too loudly.

'I don't know, Pie.'

'Let me see ... that's right! He always said that he spent too much time on the piano stool.'

'No, Lachlan and Douglas weren't in the same year at Melbourne Uni,' a woman said as she passed us. 'Not as such. But of course they knew *of* each other.'

We moved through to the auditorium and took our seats, next to Kate Stevens and a friend. 'Oh my God, I'm going to cry,' said her friend. She was tall and golden and beautiful. 'I know I'm going to cry.'

'Why?' I asked.

'Because I always cry when Douglas plays.' Her eyes welled up with tears. 'He's just so musical.'

The lights dimmed, and a wave of pre-emptive coughing passed through the hall.

'Georgie's sister went to kindergarten with Douglas in Bendigo,' a girl whispered behind us. 'And apparently he didn't have a childhood.'

When Douglas stepped out onstage, he was tall and reserved and serious in a white tuxedo, a throwback to some older code of masculinity. He bowed with a sheepish sideways smile, casually undid the top button of his suit jacket and sat at the piano to perform Stravinsky's *Petrouchka*. Mrs Sivan had said that Stravinsky did not care about the pianist, but Douglas negotiated the piece with ease. Sitting upright at the piano, cool as Cary Grant, he invoked a street scene, teeming with life: masqueraders and coachmen and grooms; a puppet in a chamber; a ballerina and a dancing bear. I leant forward in my chair, riveted by his playing, wondering if Kate's friend was crying, so that my eyes also filled with tears. The fact that I was moved moved me further, and I sobbed once, out loud. My father looked at me, surprised, and put his hand on my knee.

We drove home in silence, out of respect for the seriousness of the event. At the traffic lights at the top of O'Connell Street, my father turned to me, gravely: 'To be a concert pianist, you will have to be better than you can even imagine.'

His words hovered resonantly in the air; I nodded, accepting my mission.

'There's no need for you to hurry overseas, with Mrs Sivan here. But it's easy to be a big fish in a small pond. At some stage you will need a different environment.'

The light went green, and he started driving. I gazed out of the window at the starlit sky. *Petrouchka* was still dancing in my ears: a Moor whirred past, with an axe; a flotilla of wet nurses, dripping milk.

'Maybe you should consider Juilliard,' he continued.

'Maybe I should,' I murmured, and the street lights sped by the window like comets.

✽

The following week, Mrs Sivan left Adelaide to visit her sister in Los Angeles.

'Remember, piano always speaking, never just note-playing,' she reminded me before she went. She had charged up my Prokofiev Toccata with such dazzling energy that I was sure it would shine forever. 'It really again comes to three: why, what, how. Sometimes, you can compromise with *how* you do it, but not with *what*. And definitely never ever *why*. If you remember this, all will be excellent. Otherwise, will be awful.'

'What is *why*?'

'*Why* is basically philosophical question about why it happens. Why I want. Why the composer asks for this. But first of all, question has to be *what*. What happens here. What we talking about. What I really aim. *What what what.*'

'And what is *how*?'

'*How* you can do is highly subjective, except when composer asks you, and Prokofiev asks you exactly.'

This sounded logical; but shortly after she left, the toccata lost its charge. The piano stopped talking to me, withdrawing into itself like a reluctant bride.

'Piano chooses you,' Mrs Sivan had told me, and I had always assumed it had chosen me, as it had clearly chosen Douglas and Kate. But had it really? Or had I simply chosen it, without asking its opinion? Compared to the ease of my school subjects – quadratic equations that unravelled before my eyes, poetry that imprinted itself on my mind – playing the piano was hard work. I assumed it was like that for everybody, but was it? Sometimes Mrs Sivan told me about her students in Leningrad: 'Conservatorium only comes to cream of cream. Students there with animal abilities *you would not believe*. People who can write down full symphony, on first hearing.'

Such animal abilities lay well beyond me, and I had put her words quickly out of my mind. But now they came back to haunt me: was it possible that I lacked talent?

'Talent is like huge sum of money in bank,' she had said. 'You can spend all in ten years and – I'm sorry – default is possible. And you can't live on interest only. So much talent goes to bin, or to madhouse! Much more interesting question is what you do with your talent. Talent needs watering and constant perspective.'

In her absence, I continued to do what I could with my investment. I shore another fifteen minutes off my permitted dinner break; I took pleasure in my self-discipline, my zealotry. If the piano would not speak to me willingly, I would force it. My practice became mechanical and punitive, and playfulness again disappeared from my life.

One afternoon, as he picked me up from school, my father announced that he had invited Douglas out to lunch, to discuss study opportunities at Juilliard.

'What? *You* called up Douglas Owen?'

I couldn't believe this. How could he just call up a celebrity like that, out of the blue?

'Pie, when are you going to learn? You have to put yourself out there.'

'But that's so *embarrassing*. He wouldn't even remember us. What did he say?'

'As a matter of fact, he did remember us. He's only in Adelaide for another five days, but said he was available next Wednesday. He has an appointment in the afternoon, but he can spare an hour for lunch.'

I knew immediately that there was no appointment: that

this was the polite excuse of a chosen person, protecting his time from the unchosen.

'But I don't even want to go to Juilliard.'

'That's not what you said after his recital.'

But that was different: that was when I was intoxicated by Stravinsky, and not accountable for my actions; that was when Mrs Sivan was still around, to charge up my Prokofiev. I stared out the window as we drove past the Avenues shopping centre, busy with the errands of non-musicians.

'Sometimes I wonder if there are other things that come more naturally to me than music.' It was a large admission: a larger admission than I had ever made to myself.

My father gripped the steering wheel. 'Like what?'

'Like numbers,' I faltered. 'Or words.'

He drove in silence. 'What, you want an easy life, do you?' he muttered, as if that settled it.

The following Wednesday, my father picked me up from school, and we drove through the rain to a house in Norwood, where Douglas was staying. He came out of the front door, holding a satchel, and climbed warily into the front seat of the car.

'It's great to see you again, Doug,' said my father. 'I'm glad you could find the time.'

'Thank you for the invitation. It's very kind of you.'

'I really enjoyed your recital,' I offered, from the back seat. He didn't seem to hear me over the squawk of the windscreen wipers, so I sat in silence for the remainder of the trip, my cheeks burning.

The White Crane was almost empty when we arrived. 'Dr

Goldsworthy!' the waiter sang out, and rushed over from the bar. 'Please, your favourite table.'

He guided us to a table by the window, with a pristine tablecloth and salmon-coloured napkins folded into small crowns. I took a seat opposite Douglas. He wore a tie and a freshly ironed shirt, and seemed younger than when onstage: freckled and uncertain, even boyish.

'Did you see the game last night?' my father asked the waiter. 'That centre-forward – what a drama queen! Deserved an Oscar.'

Outside the window, pedestrians struggled past with umbrellas, dodging puddles, taking shelter under awnings. How carefree they were, even without realising it! The rain might be uncomfortable, but it was rarely embarrassing.

'It needs to be a turbo-banquet,' my father chuckled to the waiter, 'because our friend here has an appointment to get to. Actually, I don't know if you've met. Benny, this is the concert pianist Douglas Owen.'

'For distinguished guest, no problem,' Benny said and returned to the kitchen.

Douglas stared intently at the tablecloth. I tried subliminally to communicate that I had no ideas above my station, and that I would never seriously consider a move to Juilliard.

'So Doug, as you might know, Anna was awarded the 1989 Thelma Dent Memorial Prize and the 1990 Adelaide Eisteddfod Yamaha Medallion for Most Promising Pianist.'

'*Dad!*' I kicked him under the table. Didn't he know who he was talking to? Douglas was a prizewinner at the *Concorso Pianistico Internazionale Città di Senigallia*.

'That's excellent news,' Douglas said. 'Congratulations.'

'She's learning an enormous amount from Mrs Sivan, and has no intention of leaving Adelaide for some time.'

'Mrs Sivan is a very special lady. Please give her my most affectionate regards.'

'But at some later stage we thought study at Juilliard might be worth considering.'

I glared at him. *Not we. You! Only you!*

'That's a good idea.' Douglas reached into his satchel and passed me a Juilliard syllabus. There was a picture of a clown on its cover, in kindergarten colours: blue, red, yellow. 'It's a little out of date, but I don't think too much has changed.'

I grasped the syllabus gratefully and turned to the list of piano faculty, weighing each name silently in my mouth: *Bella Davidovich, Herbert Stessin, Joseph Kalichstein.* They were hefty, satisfying names; perhaps I could construct a wall out of them, and block out the awful events unfolding around me.

'That reminds me, I thought you might be interested in this.' My father passed him his book. 'It's my novel *Maestro.* Just out in paperback. Inspired in part by Mrs Sivan.'

'That's extremely kind of you.'

Silence, except for the muted strains of 'Somewhere Over the Rainbow' on vibraphone. I sensed my father trying to catch my eye, urging me to speak. *Jacob Lateiner, Emanuel Ax, Seymour Lipkin.*

'We saw an interesting interview recently with the pianist Susanna Parnell,' he continued gamely. 'She spoke of how intimidating it was to walk down the corridor at Juilliard, listening to the standard of everyone practising around you.'

'Absolutely,' said Douglas. 'The standard is very high. But

then again, that's New York, and that's Juilliard. That's why you're there.'

The food arrived: rice-paper rolls, salt-and-pepper squid, stir-fry vegetables, fried rice. I reached for my knife and fork, but abandoned them when Douglas picked up his chopsticks.

'I'm sure Anna also has questions for you,' my father prompted.

I panicked. Memory lapse. What sort of questions did people ask each other? I opened my mouth, hoping something would come out: 'What's the weather like in New York?'

'At this time of year, it can be terribly hot. I was glad to be in Adelaide, but with weather like today I'm not so sure.'

We laughed uproariously.

'Do you enjoy living in New York?' I continued, encouraged.

'Very much. Only I don't see as much of it as I'd like to, because of the demands of practice. You would know about that.'

'Exactly!'

'What repertoire are you working on?' he asked.

'Oh, a Chopin ballade or two. The Prokofiev Toccata.'

He nodded, thoughtfully. 'Serious repertoire.'

'What was it like auditioning for Juilliard?'

'Terrifying. You fly all the way around the world, and they only hear a tiny part of your program. You have ten minutes to prove yourself.'

As I tried to think of my next question, I stopped concentrating on my chopsticks, and a piece of squid flew out of them as if from a sling-shot. It pinged off Douglas's tie with slapstick precision, ricocheted off his glass of water, and landed on the white tablecloth in front of him, where it sat, unrepentant.

My father laughed.

'Sorry,' I attempted, but my voice had evaporated.

'No problem,' Douglas said. He continued eating, but did not venture any more questions, while the rain outside became louder.

'You mentioned you had an appointment,' my father said eventually.

'That's right, I did!'

My father fixed up the bill, and then we ran outside through the rain to the car, and coursed through the streets of Norwood.

Douglas cleared his throat. 'Just here would be fine, thank you.'

'Not in this weather!' my father insisted, gallantly. 'We'll drive you all the way.'

He steered the car into the next street and parked outside a fine old bluestone house. Douglas thanked us for lunch and wished me all the best for my musical future. Then he stepped out of the car, lingered for a moment under a tree, and launched himself into the rain, sprinting back towards the corner.

We watched, bewildered.

'I'm a drongo!' my father wailed suddenly. 'It's the wrong bloody street, but he was too polite to say anything.'

He performed a quick U-turn and sped after him, blaring the horn, but Douglas continued running, without looking back.

Finally I put my hand on my father's arm: 'I think we should leave him alone now.'

We pulled over to the curb and watched Douglas recede into the rain, and then vanish entirely. I knew his appointment was with the piano, and I envied him the simplicity of this: a chosen person, returning to that which had chosen him.

❀

A month later, Mrs Sivan returned from America, and enlisted me again in the chosen people. Now that she was back, the piano keyboard was again my playground, through which I flew, weightless, hand-in-hand with Prokofiev, defying God's laws and scripting my own. Part of the rapture of the toccata was in the playing of it: its relentless drive, the thrill of its improbability. I sprang from point to point, deft as a tightrope walker, with all those possible wrong notes grinning below. There was no room here for anxieties about talent, which now seemed foolishly self-obsessed. Instead, I summoned up all those niggling voices – those petty-minded gossipers, those chattering doubts – and blazed them into the air with a blare of trombones.

With the help of Mrs Sivan and Prokofiev, everything was easy, and I moved through my list of goals, ticking them off one by one. I won the important sections at the Adelaide Eisteddfod; I gave two successful recitals for the Australian Society for Keyboard Music.

'The biggest thing is that we are all coming to serving,' she reminded me. 'Like Shostakovich says, we are all soldiers. But of course is good to want to be a general! I never say no to ambition. We all go, step by step, but our aim always *creation*, never ego or narcissism.'

At school speech night, in the Adelaide Town Hall, I was

named dux of the school, and awarded the prizes for music and English and mathematics and history and debating. Each time my name was read out, I felt it as a small caress, polishing my inner sheen after the ravages of adolescence. The following week, at the Leavers' Dinner, I was asked to make the toast.

'As I leave this hallowed institution, I feel crippled by nostalgia. Why must high school ever end?'

It was an act of revenge on five years of high school: on the cool kids, with their impenetrable codes; on the doubting teachers, who counselled me to become doctor or lawyer; on my classmates, who refused to take my calling seriously: *Why don't you give me your brains, while you fiddle away at the keyboard?*

'And finally I'd like to thank the principal for coming to our debates.' My duxhood glowed around me like a protective force-field. 'He was in fact our secret weapon. By sleeping through them, he gave us real incentive, as we tried desperately to wake him and secure his attention.'

It gained the easy laughs I was seeking even as it made no allowance for the fine teachers who had taken me under their wing: the Mrs Athersmiths, the Mr Clarkes. I was a young revolutionary, in love with my own powers. *You can't make an omelette without breaking eggs.* Of course there would be dissonances: I was emancipated in spirit, and I was going to make a huge impression.

PART III.

Chapter 11. Bach

ONE MORNING IN JANUARY, as I waited for my results by the letterbox, my mother came running outside with the telephone: 'It's the Senior Secondary Assessment Board!'

I took the phone from her, listened gravely to what the man had to say, and hung up.

'It looks like I received perfect scores in all subjects.'

'Yippee-dippee-dippee-doo!'

'It's certainly a relief,' I conceded, as she hugged me, but I felt queasy. There was something extravagant about these results: something over the top. Had I gone too far this time? Could such excess cost me the Tennyson Medal or the Don Maynard Prize?

The phone began ringing with requests for interviews, and my mother drove me into the offices of the *Advertiser* newspaper, where I jumped into the air for the camera alongside the other top students. *Yippee*, I prompted myself, *Hip hip hooray!* Later that afternoon, a Channel 7 news crew came to our front door. 'I was sure I messed up my music and English exams,' I told them, reassuring the universe of my humility. 'I'm afraid I might be using up all my luck,' I confided to Radio SAFM.

A week later, I received a second phone call, saying that I had won the Tennyson Medal and the Don Maynard Prize, sharing each prize with a different girl. I called my father at work. He was silent for several seconds. 'Fuck,' he whispered. Then I went to see Mrs Sivan. 'Is *excellent* news!' she declared, leading me triumphantly into her music room, where she was teaching an ear, nose and throat surgeon. 'This girl received full marks for Year 12 *and* Don Maynard Prize for best music student *and* Tennyson Medal.'

The doctor stood and shook my hand. 'Congratulations.'

'I never pressured this girl to become musician. Made own choice completely. Could do anything, and chose piano. Makes me very happy and very proud, because music needs her. Why?'

He looked uncertain.

'Because music is the life, music is the health of a nation! We have *huge* responsibility to future! A responsibility of giving, of passing this human spirit to next generations.' She was singing now, her eyes dancing with evangelical fervour. 'Music *so* important! Can give so much to young people. And is *crucial* for general future. This spiritual excitement and knowledge has very concrete knowledge behind it, is *very* precise science. Music itself can't change whole world, but definitely can change us, one person at a time.'

I showed them my academic transcript, with its five 20s lined up neatly in a column: proof against all disaster, more powerful than any Fibonacci sequence. And now I had two prizes, with names like incantations: the *Don Maynard Prize*, the *Tennyson Medal*. Surely these guaranteed something – endless future happiness and success?

The following day I went into the *Advertiser* for an interview with the other Tennyson Medallist, Priya Vigneswaran. We were photographed on the steps of the Mortlock Library, hugging each other, our heads thrown back in laughter, our teeth glinting in the sun.

'That's it girls, that's gorgeous. Just like models. Perfection.'

Afterwards, Priya told the journalist that she planned to study medicine; I explained that I was going to be a concert pianist.

'Do you have to move elsewhere to do that?'

'Basically you tour the world.'

'Yes, but can you be based in Adelaide?'

I realised I had no clear idea of what concert pianists did, beyond giving the occasional concert. How frequently did they perform? Where did they live?

'I think so. But eventually I might move somewhere else.'

'Like where?'

Nearby, children splashed in the museum fountain, full of holiday laughter. I gazed at them wistfully, as a model might, and hazarded a guess: 'Sydney?'

Priya said her mother had taught her to read before she started school; I pointed out that my kindergarten teacher, Mrs Hackett, had done the same. I mentioned Mrs Sivan in passing, but did not thank my family, or any of the teachers at my school.

The article appeared the following day: *Anna plans to move to Sydney to seek fame and fortune as a concert pianist. She attributes all of her success to her kindergarten teacher, who taught her how to read.*

The phone began ringing with another round of congratulations. 'I remember a conversation we had some time ago, in which I suggested that knowledge is power,' my grandfather chuckled. 'Your grandmother and I are very proud of you, darling.'

A final call came through before lunch. 'Anna, it's me.' Mrs Sivan's voice lacked its customary warmth. 'I learn very interesting thing today. I learn in the newspaper that you will move to Sydney.'

I felt instantly ashamed of my behaviour at the Mortlock Library: vamping on the steps, boasting of my childhood precocity and exotic career plans.

'Not really. Or only maybe.'

'Very strange article, of course. *She attributes all of her success to her kindergarten teacher.* Of course, Mum and Dad and nobody else taught you anything.'

I realised that her name had been omitted from the article. 'I mentioned your name, but the reporter left it out!'

'What I need my name in newspaper for? For me it's not important. But important for *you* to learn importance of gratitude, of acknowledging roots. Is very easy to take people for granted.'

Her greatness was a premise of my musical life: it seemed as little in need of acknowledgment as a mountain needed acknowledgment of its size.

'But I don't take you for granted.'

'Of course. And of course you must go to Sydney immediately.'

In the past, she had told me stories about clashes with students: the girl who said she was beyond Chopin; the woman who boasted that she was better than Richter: 'Very good, then, we will change your interpretation immediately.' And afterwards the protests. 'What is problem? Richter can change his interpretation a million times. Depends on feelings of day.' She told me these stories as lessons in humility and gratitude, and from my privileged position in her heart I had laughed at such students, at their hubris and necessary comeuppance. But now, as she wished me goodbye over the phone, the warmth and safety vanished from my world, and I ran into my father's study, distraught: 'I think Mrs Sivan just fired me.'

He drove me to see her, and as I gazed out of the window, the route to her house had a valedictory quality: aloof, alien, as though it had already moved on. For the first time I properly considered everything she had done for me: the hours she had sat next to that nine-year-old, and later that thirteen-year-old, and now this seventeen-year-old, explaining things not once, not twice, but again and again; the ideas she flung at me each week, profligate, in the hope that one or two might stick; the work of art, the *act of creation*, that was each of her lessons. She could be performing on any stage in the world, teaching in any conservatorium, but instead she was here, in a suburban house in Adelaide, performing for an audience of two, as she guided me towards music, note by note, sound by sound. By the time we arrived at her house, I was overcome by shame, matched only by fear of what was about to happen. I knocked on her front door, my pulse throbbing in my ears, primed for reprimand. But when she answered, she just looked tired. I had never seen her vulnerable before, and it shocked me.

'I'm sorry.'

She studied my face, warily, and I realised she was a human being, after all.

'I really appreciate all you have done for me.'

She shrugged. 'Sometimes I think what I doing for students fantastic, and sometimes not. Sometimes people value things more when they have to fight for it.'

'But I do value you. I'm so grateful for all you have given me.'

I lacked the emotional vocabulary for this sort of declaration, and the words sounded insincere, but they were not.

'Of course. When you're strong enough, you can always say thanks. But when you pretend to be, you insecure – is more difficult.'

She gestured us in, and we followed her over to the piano, where the offending article was displayed on the music stand. 'Altogether, you make yourself look very cheap. *Anna seeks fame and fortune as a concert pianist ...*'

'I didn't say I wanted fame and fortune. I just said I wanted to be a concert pianist.'

'Even to say it. Life in music *much* broader. Must be concert pianist *and* concert teacher. Concert teacher in many ways higher than concert pianist: you have to be concert pianist first, and then be able to pass it on. We have huge responsibility. *Huge.* For passing this legacy. Never just about ego. Always music first.'

'I know.'

'Never about keeping music for yourself. Always about yourself in music.'

'I know, I'm sorry.'

'Please, no tears.' She took my hand now. 'Is very good lesson, really. You have right to make mistake, and grow. But you are not schoolgirl any more. From now on needs be *much* more intelligent.'

As we left, she embraced me, and I felt restored to the fold, but provisionally, with no sense of tenure. Things were more complicated than I had hoped; a perfect score was not, after all, proof against disaster.

❀

Now that school had ended, I felt an immense yearning for real life, or what I imagined it to be: the endless recreation of the non-musicians of the world. Summer beckoned with new prospects: the sudden recklessness of alcohol, men's eyes catching mine as I danced at the pub. I spent balmy evenings drinking margaritas with Sophia; I lay in the Botanic Gardens with Sam, while the sun moved across the sky, baking the earth beneath us. Somewhere else, the day's practice hours dwindled to nothing; there was a wantonness in ignoring them, in forgetting to count.

The following day, I practised twice as long, to make up for it. 'That's a beautiful song,' Sam said, when my mother brought the phone into the music room. 'What's it called?'

It was Bach's C-sharp Major Prelude and Fugue from Book One, but I steered the conversation away. I didn't want to talk about music with him; I didn't know how to. On Valentine's Day, I stayed the night at his house, and woke the next morning to the soft motor of his breathing. He had given me a Paddington Bear; looking at it now, so sturdy and self-absorbed, I felt a rising panic. Why wasn't I practising? How had I allowed my head to be turned? I got up quickly and caught the bus home with my furry charge. It had a baggage tag around its neck: *Please look after this bear. Thank you.* More responsibility!

'Is everything okay?' he asked over the phone. 'You seemed a bit distant when you left.'

'Everything's fine,' I said, and returned to my practice of Bach. I was now preparing the A-minor Prelude and Fugue from Book One, with its grand, exultant ending, the sudden illumination of the major. 'For Bach, all endings are happy,' Mrs Sivan had told me. 'Why? Because he is deeply religious in belief. Brings full peace: peace of contact, of surroundings, of support, of communications, and of respect. Schumann says *make Bach your daily bread and you will surely become fine musician!* Must learn new prelude and fugue every week.'

I stopped returning Sam's calls and addressed myself instead to Bach. Later, when Mrs Sivan told me to address my Rachmaninov to someone personal, I thought of him, but now I felt only relief. Each morning, I stepped out of bed into a prelude and fugue, where each voice understood each other, where relationships were harmonious, where endings were always happy.

At the Elder Conservatorium, I made new friends who were also musicians. Monica was a flautist, disciplined and poised as a dancer; Leah was a sultry cellist; Helen was the exuberant violinist with whom I had shared the Don Maynard Prize. They knew what it was to practise all day, to make sacrifices for their art. And while they didn't view their vocation in quite the mythic terms I viewed mine, we understood each other. We used a code of acronyms to talk about the orchestras they played in – AYO, ASO, AdCO – and if non-musicians were present, we made little effort to translate.

My scheduled piano lessons at the conservatorium lasted for forty-five minutes, but Mrs Sivan saw me at least twice a week, for three or four hours. 'What can you do in forty-five minutes?' she asked. 'Listen to student play, say *very good, bye-bye, see you next week*. Real work impossible! In Russia, we have at least two-hour lesson on piano *alone*. Then after, another eight hours of professional learning: piano solo, piano duo, piano accompaniment, chamber music. Difficult really for me to give you all this, but we try.'

Over the years of my theory lessons with Debra, I had received a thorough grounding in harmony; now, at the conservatorium, I discovered special new chords: the doubly augmented sixth, with its bracing outward thrust; the tasty Neapolitan, a flat second chord in first inversion. I enjoyed the mathematics of musical analysis, the possibilities it offered of getting things correct and right: a V^4_2 chord must resolve to a I^6, because the seventh in the bass must fall, QED. But in my lessons with Mrs Sivan, these equations took on a new life. Understanding chord progressions was not enough: they had to add up to meaning. 'What is the difference between A flat, here, and now transformed to G sharp? Exactly! New hope, new future, new perspective!' Each harmony had its own gravitational pull or push; like the periodic table, chords ranged from the unstable to the inert. She deconstructed each phrase, reducing melodic lines to their essence; years later, when I encountered the advanced theory of Schenkerian analysis, I realised that this is what she had taught me.

At the conservatorium, we studied the lives of the great composers, but in my piano lessons, she took me into their inner lives, reading their music as autobiography, until they became more real than many of the people in my life. 'What is different in Bach's sense of the God?' she asked, as we worked on the Prelude and Fugue in C-sharp Minor from Book One. 'Some using religious to save, some as anchor, some for discussion, some for fighting, and some for possibility: *only in bad times I need to say maybe.* But Bach was deeply religious man, for whom God was natural. All church was telling to be afraid, but Bach told, *why I have to be afraid of my father? I want to communicate with him.* He constantly brings father to his home, and constantly discussing all his problems with him.'

＊

Now that I had my driver's licence, my father no longer accompanied me to lessons. Sometimes Mrs Sivan asked after him, a little wistfully, but he was writing a novel about bestiality and had moved on to new obsessions. In his absence, our relationship changed. When I arrived at her house, she would invite me into the kitchen for a coffee, Vienna-style, double-strength, flavoured with cinnamon. 'I still believe strongly in a cup of coffee a day, despite everybody says. And this dark chocolate fantastic. Please, take! Natural drugs. We do huge job, need enormous energy.'

As I feasted on chocolate and coffee, she improvised great speeches about music, or human relations, or international politics: 'They say Russia only country with unpredictable past,' she laughed, and moved on to reminiscences about the stage: 'When you play concerto with best orchestra, best conductor, is greatest joy. Full love affair. It gives you wings, full freedom! Believe me, you will fly!'

I hoped I would. I was nearly eighteen and had never played a concerto with a professional orchestra; I felt anxious about leaving my first time too late. Any large group of people was intimidating, but an orchestra was even worse: a large group of professional musicians, each nursing a private opinion of your playing. Imagine having a memory lapse in front of an orchestra! Imagine the conductor calling a halt to proceedings: that loaded silence, the loud beating of your heart as the audience looked on, aghast.

'Our relationship now changing,' she said to me one day. 'Forever you will feel huge respect, of course, but now comes more to level of friendship. *Mrs Sivan* too formal, now that you are adult. You can call me Eleonora.' I struggled with the presumption of this, but coached myself to use her first name, even as she remained the more respectful Mrs Sivan in my head.

At the piano, we remained teacher and student, coursing through the repertoire more quickly than ever before, until I was scaling its virtuoso summits: Liszt's *Mephisto Waltz*, Brahms' *Variations on a Theme of Paganini*, Ravel's *Gaspard de la Nuit*. I alternated between moments of lucidity, in which I could hear everything she asked for, and absent-mindedness, in which I looped through my repertoire on autopilot. 'Not,' she repeated, bringing me back to the present. 'Must listen. Must miss not one detail.'

One Tuesday, as I drove to my lesson, I was rehearsing a Chopin nocturne in my head for a recital on the weekend. I came to the corner my grandfather had pointed out for me, all those years before: *We now approach Ascot Avenue, elsewhere known as Portrush Road. At this point we undertake a right-hand turn.* There was an enharmonic change in the Chopin nocturne that I could almost feel, but not quite: the way it gathered a D flat and transformed it into a C sharp, changing the bass line's direction. I tried again to experience it, and the light turned yellow, and I undertook the right-hand turn.

My Chopin was interrupted by a great clash of cymbals and crunch of metal; the seatbelt clamped tight on my bones as I watched the universe spin fast around me. I felt wonder, and then outrage: *Someone must have driven into me! How rude!* When the car stopped spinning, I kicked open the door and stumbled into the intersection, which was hushed as an auditorium. My car was smoking, and squashed flat; I could see that it was completely written off. A woman emerged from an undented Holden Tarago. 'My husband's in hospital,' she seemed to be saying. 'I wouldn't usually go through a yellow light.'

I lay down on a nature strip, and a policeman rode up on a motorbike, wearing aviator glasses and a white helmet. He throbbed his engine – 'That's going to cost you three demerit points' – and zoomed off. It dawned on me that I was the one at fault, that this catastrophe was the result of my heedlessness, my failure to pay attention, my failure to *listen*. A woman invited me into her house, where she poured me a glass of water and lent me her phone. 'Dad,' I sobbed, and then he was there, and I realised it was difficult to breathe, and could someone please call Mrs Sivan and apologise that I was running late.

I did not make it to my lesson that day. Instead, I spent most of the next week in bed, nursing my injuries and my shame. Lurking in my consciousness was the knowledge of what could have been: a knowledge I tiptoed towards, and then retreated from. I had come to believe that everything was a lesson, that the world arranged itself for the purpose of my education, but where was the lesson in this?

'They say you should get back on the horse as soon as you can,' my mother reminded me, but I resolved not to get on that particular horse again. Instead, four days later, I climbed out of bed and went to the piano. I had whiplash, and bruises all over my torso in giant abstract splashes of colour, but my recital was only two days away, and there was work to do. 'Of course music is healing arts,' Mrs Sivan said, 'but please, my darling, no playing through pain.' But I felt no pain when I was playing, only when I stopped, and I needed to bring Bach into my home, to right things.

Onstage that Sunday, with my bruises concealed, playing a concert seemed at once more and less serious than it had before. It was safer to drive a piano than a car; the repercussions of a concentration lapse were nowhere near as severe. But the universe had expanded downwards, and upwards: there was more capacity for pain than I cared to admit, and the solace of Bach's music was consequently much greater. I had been initiated into a darker, parallel reality, and in the Chopin nocturne I let myself go there, bringing it to the quietest place I could find inside me, and I felt the audience come too.

'You had that audience wrapped around your finger,' my father said afterwards as he gave me a painful hug.

'*Much* more musical,' Mrs Sivan declared. 'Many things different from how I would do, but this only subjective. And this is good – I never say do like me only. Becoming more and more artistic.'

Such words were rare from her, but I still felt chastened from the accident, and resolved to pay better attention.

Chapter 12. Rachmaninov

Mrs Sivan's words about teaching continued to haunt me: 'We have huge responsibility to future! Of passing this spirit to next generations. Always remember: only what you give is yours.' Several of her students ran music schools of their own, regularly bringing their students to her for 'consultations', so that she oversaw an army of Adelaide's young pianists.

'Not all students will be professional pianist,' she conceded, 'but equally important to educate audiences. In some ways teaching is highest calling. Because must be able to *do*, first, but then translate into words. And sometimes what we try to explain is so – what is this word? – elusive. Like tiny fish in your palm, you catch, and then – boom! – it *jump* out of your hand.'

I took on a handful of private piano students, and began teaching at Debra's piano school. Initially I felt liberated in the teacher's chair. At one remove from the piano stool, away from the distractions of playing, I was forced to listen, and I experienced the clarity of the conductor. But somehow, as I tried to communicate this clarity to my students, that tiny fish flicked in my hand, and then disappeared.

'I thought you told me not to sit,' a ten-year-old girl protested.

'Yes – but that doesn't mean you should ignore punctuation.'

She looked at me dubiously. 'Didn't you say Bach never stops?'

'Yes,' I faltered, 'but we should still observe phrasing.'

Was this the way I would serve Mrs Sivan's legacy? Scrambling her message, from one telling to the next, as in a childhood game of Chinese whispers?

'How did you teach me?' I asked her one day, in desperation. I had been there, of course, but aspects of the process seemed inexplicable, almost mystical. It was one thing to speak about style and meaning and logic, to discuss the *what* and the *why*. But how did you convey the *how*? How did you transfer a physical knowledge from your hands to the hands of another?

'Sometimes I don't know myself,' she smiled. 'But important always to touch hands, to *emancipate* them. At same time, be careful not to demonstrate too much: children very good at copy. Many teachers teach by *do it my way*, teaching only for today. Very good, but then student handicapped for tomorrow. You must prepare students for life.'

I attempted to remake myself in her image: extending my one-hour lessons indefinitely, packing them with lecture and anecdote, and passing on her expressions, like the most ardent of disciples.

'Is nothing ever good enough for you?' a teenage boy protested.

'My compliment is to sit and work,' I replied, hoping he could not hear the quotation marks. 'You need more *garmonic* sense.'

'What?'

I corrected myself, but the word *harmonic* seemed ineffectual by comparison.

'Of course teaching gift needs generosity and *huge* hours,' she acknowledged. 'Some pianists playing – yes, I heard – incredible! But ask them what they doing and they can't explain, because completely unconscious. Someone told me was impossible to teach this, but *is* possible. Of course, can never guarantee results: never know who will get and who will not.'

I riffed for hours to my students about composers and sound production and hands, variations on what she had told me and improvisations of my own, metaphors that surprised me as they escaped my mouth and then vanished forever. My students' eyes slid to the clock and back again; they dabbed at their faces, removing the enthusiastic flecks of my saliva; when I released them out the front door, they gasped gratefully at the air, as if reborn.

'Very important to know measure,' she told me. 'Too much, and immediately they intimidated. Too little, and no point. Psychology *very* important. Always remember: individual human being, and respect to person sitting near you. You must be light in student's life.'

❋

Compared to teaching, performing seemed less complicated. I only had to tell one person what to do, and increasingly she obeyed. I accepted every invitation that came my way, performing for Probus societies and music clubs, at choir concerts and fundraisers, in historical houses and in town halls. Some mornings, my father came into my bedroom with the newspaper and a cup of tea, to read me my latest review. 'You shouldn't read your reviews, you should measure them,' he would begin, as I laughed impatiently.

At this stage, the critics were usually kind, and I felt relieved not to be censured, but little pleasure beyond that. I had taken Mrs Sivan's words to heart about the unreliability of opinion; increasingly, the only person I sought to please was her. But this became more difficult all the time. As soon as I had grasped a truth about a piece, she demanded more. 'Life in music always deeper, always more doors opening. Now you can take more, immediately I give more.'

Despite my busy concert schedule, I had still not performed a piano concerto. I knew I had to find a willing orchestra and confront my fears, but this was not easy, and Mrs Sivan advised me to avoid the amateur: 'Playing with good orchestra is greatest joy. But playing with bad orchestra absolute waste of time. Even worse, can *kill* your sounds.'

I decided to enter the ABC Young Performers Awards, a national competition in which finalists performed with one of the major ABC orchestras. The first two rounds comprised auditions before a selection panel, and I spent the summer holidays preparing my program. In February, my father dropped me at the ABC building in Collinswood. After signing in at security, I followed its beige corridors to a small foyer outside Studio 520, where I waited outside the spiral staircase, reapplying my lipstick until it tasted like mud.

A silver-haired adjudicator came to the door. 'The jury is ready for you.' He beckoned me into the studio, and introduced me to his colleagues. 'What would you like to play first?'

'The Chopin nocturne.'

I registered a supercilious eyebrow and sat down at the piano, making myself quiet, to get a sense of the space.

An adjudicator cleared his throat. 'When you're ready.'

I had not played this particular Steinway before, but when I embraced the opening, it reached back to me like an old friend, and I felt an immediate relief. As I introduced the right-hand melody, I listened to what the *sounds told me after*, sending them out to the walls and bringing them back in, until I felt I was mapping the studio through sonar, feeling it in my fingers like a type of Braille. *This is going well.* Banish that thought! *But it is. Does that mean a memory lapse is overdue?* I ignored the voices in my head and concentrated on Chopin, trailing these sounds across the kinks in the ceiling and over the softening, undefended faces of the adjudicators, until the final chord, which hung in the air for a moment and then evaporated, leaving a shimmer in the room.

'Thank you.'

'Yes, thank you very much *indeed*.'

'What would you like to hear next, Harold?'

'Any of it, really. But perhaps – let's say – Stravinsky.'

I launched into 'Shrovetide Fair' from *Petrouchka* and claimed its exuberance as my own, celebrating the fact that such moments existed, when my hands and ears and head and heart were in perfect alignment, with the universe cartwheeling around them. Afterwards, there was a flurry of handshakes, supportive nods and gallant openings of the door, and later that afternoon, a thrilling phone call from the ABC: 'The judges were very impressed.'

The second round of auditions called for the performance of a complete concerto, accompanied by a second piano playing the orchestra part. I had nominated Rachmaninov's Second Concerto, which he composed after being treated with hypnosis: his therapist, Dr Dahl, had predicted that he would emerge from depression and write a great work. It was my favourite concerto, and I had written it down on the application form with a flourish, flattered that such a piece might belong to me. But it had seemed like tempting fate to begin preparing it until I was definitely through to the second round; now, as I divided its ninety-one pages into the four weeks remaining before the audition, I started to panic.

'Do you think I should pull out?' I asked Mrs Sivan at my next lesson.

'Impossible. Then they never ask you back. We work hard, and Rachmaninov so great pianist, he make it easy. You will very like.'

She opened the thick score to the first movement. 'Rachmaninov so generous, so cultivated and self-sustained. And always bells. Bells can be many: church bells, sleigh bells, but these are bells of life. Altogether Rachmaninov extremely positive, extremely healthy composer. This is music of health and balance, very giving and healing. Exact opposite to Scriabin in this way. And of course, Chopin's influence huge.'

'How?'

She thought about this. 'His music very honest and very philosophical, very emotional but with great objective quality.' She leant into the piano and wrapped her hands around a chord. 'And like Chopin he embrace piano. What you think, Rachmaninov not one of greatest pianists of all time?'

'Of course.'

'So great that his technique basically not exist as technique, only as improvising. You find interval and you conduct.'

I reached for the piano.

'Not!' she called out, before I even played the first chord. I caught her eye, and we both laughed.

'Remember?'

I quoted her from my first lesson, all those years before: *'You do not need to play anything, your hands are wrong.'*

'Of course! Because music start already, inside. Watch sometimes people, see how much they say unconsciously, with body language. Only enormous strange spy can hide it: *genius* spy. We start again.'

We worked on the great gongs of the opening, listening to the changes in overtones between each chord, their growing resonance, before the explosive entrance of the first theme. 'Exactly! This is swimming in sounds! In life continuing! Remember freedom of hearing is based on only one thing: *full* understanding of what you're doing. And only then, you're free to create anything you like.'

At home, I lost that freedom of hearing. I became fixated on memory, on swotting those ninety-one pages of music, ignoring the sounds in my obsession with the notes. At night, as I fell asleep, I saw the imprints of the notes on the inside of my eyelids; in the morning, when I awoke, I felt the third movement in the muscles of my jaw, where I had been grinding my teeth.

'Not. This I don't like. Your sounds in cages. Must be free, like birds. Exactly! And what about rhythm? You take strict rhythm in pushing, in dictating, in metronomic. Time must be precise, of course, because you must play with orchestra, but at same time very stretching, very giving. What is the difference between solo part and orchestral part?'

'The individual versus the mass?'

'Of course. Large group of people never that flexible.' She demonstrated the opening theme in the orchestral part. 'Even in Rachmaninov, with full emotional outpouring, large group of people has *much* more objective sound. Now same theme as soloist.'

This time, her sound was lit from within, incandescent as a single human mind. She laughed as I recognised the difference.

'Much more personal, of course! Soloist has full individualistic freedom, enormous flexibility, enormous subjectivity, full emancipation, but always *inside brackets*. And even though brackets exist, nobody pay attention. Always remember: *time is emotionally emancipated*.'

In her lessons, we escaped the brackets of time, but at home, the clock continued. Only three weeks remained before the audition, and I had only memorised one movement. I stopped taking breaks except to eat, and only then when necessary; after hours of practice, when I glanced away from the score, notes floated in the air around me, like stars.

'This section like – how do you say? – little small things, glittering ...'

'Like glitter?'

'Exactly!'

'I think I understand.'

'But understand itself not enough. Must be able to *do*, first, and then repeat and repeat and repeat until two hundred per cent secure.'

I practised this glittering passagework at home, listening to the connection between every sound, and then repeated the same two lines again and again and again, until I was on an endless merry-go-round of glitter and the world contracted around me and my peripheral vision disappeared. After one hour – or was it two? – I heard a squirmy voice in the room, addressing me urgently. I stopped playing and looked around, readjusting my eyes to the light. Silence. When I returned to that passage, the voice started up again, even more frantically: *yakkedy yakkedy yak!* It had nothing to do with the concerto, but came from somewhere between the notes: a gatecrasher to Rachmaninov. I could not quite gauge its meaning, only its breathless, busybody intonation. Unnerved, I took a tea break and watched the minute hand of the clock propel me closer to my moment of reckoning.

The following morning, I went to my first rehearsal with my accompanist, Inna. She was also a student of Mrs Sivan's, recently arrived from Russia, and I felt safe with her, and my gatecrasher left us alone. We began the first movement, and I tasted the thrill of concerto playing. Then I took a wrong turn in the development and was dumped into a memory lapse.

'Once more, yes?' she said, blinking eagerly.

This time I forgot about memory and submitted to the music's gorgeous abandon. I grabbed those giant fistfuls of notes and tossed them to Inna; she lobbed them back to me, their chromaticism glistening in the air like coins. After the abrupt ending, we turned to each other and grinned. 'Will be beautiful,' she said. Based on this rehearsal, there was a fifty per cent chance that she was right.

'Always remember, must have *absolute inside freedom!*' Mrs Sivan said in my final lesson before the audition. 'Very sad to say, really, but today a lot of young people already dead from inside, before physically dead. And when you dead inside, *immediately* your sounds are dead. Life in sounds need constant source inside you, like hills water.'

The following afternoon, I arrived at Studio 520 with Inna and her page-turner. 'And this young lady is Anna Goldsworthy,' said an adjudicator, introducing me to the national judge.

'Enchanted.'

Did he really say that? I sat at the piano and turned to Inna, who winked at me. There had not been a South Australian keyboard finalist for several years; the hopes of everyone in the state were riding on me, even if they didn't realise it. As I rang those opening gongs, I forgot about life in sounds, and tried instead to calculate my security percentage, as though I were being judged on a feat of memory alone. Had it crept upwards since my first rehearsal, to sixty per cent, perhaps, or even seventy? *You need to be inside brackets, of course, but absolutely emancipated.* Inna entered with the orchestral theme, and I let its assurance guide me, forgetting about percentages, concentrating only on the music. *Even though brackets exist, nobody pay attention.* Things were going well until I arrived at the squirmy passage that had once talked to me, where I heard an outraged rustle of papers from the jury. There was a loud, emphatic whisper: 'Preposterous.' I ignored it, and continued my earnest song, but now another adjudicator joined in the whispering, and then another. They repeated the same word to each other, over and over – *preposterous, preposterous* – until it became a soundtrack of muttering throughout the performance, subject to the music's *accelerandos* and *ritardandos*, concentrated on these plosive 'p's, which matched the consonant frontal edge of the piano's sounds, that attack of hammer hitting string. Even as I aimed to create a *cantabile* sound, camouflaging that edge into the vowels of song, this muttering of *preposterous* bound me to the notes, until I too seemed to be playing the word *preposterous*, performing my own indictment.

Afterwards, there were no supportive nods or thank yous, and I had to open the door myself as we left.

'They were so rude!' I gasped in the foyer.

'What you mean by this?' Inna asked.

'Didn't you hear? They kept on saying *preposterous!*'

'I do not understand. What is this word?'

Inna's page-turner looked at me. 'I could see them, and nobody spoke through the entire performance.'

I drove home, confused. Was it possible that, by trying to cram-learn this concerto, I had reversed its healing powers? That this glorious work, which marked Rachmaninov's return to health, had become the agent of my undoing?

When I arrived, my parents greeted me with expectant smiles.

'It was a disaster.'

'Is this a case of hyperbolitis?' my mother asked, on her way out to bridge.

My father ordered us take-away Thai that night, which was my favourite, and borrowed a video, *Zorba the Greek*. I knew he was trying to make me feel better, but the sticky rice had no taste, and I could spare no sympathy for the widow in the film.

'Stop being self-indulgent, Pie,' he said.

I considered running to my bedroom and slamming the door: technically, I was still a teenager. But I was too exhausted for extreme acts. Instead, I stared catatonically at the black and white figures flickering on the screen. Despite glimpses of success, failure seemed to be my default setting, my true home; I knew I would never play with an orchestra; I was not only preposterous but insane.

Chapter 13. Beethoven

'WHAT IS THE DIFFERENCE between good and great pianist?' Mrs Sivan often asked.

'I don't know – what?' This response seemed rhythmically necessary, like a knock-knock joke.

'Little bits.' She chuckled. '*Little bit* more hearing, *little bit* more understanding, *little bit* more logic in fantasy, *little bit* more fantasy in logic. Do you understand how little bits? But these little bits take whole lifetime.'

As a child I struggled to understand these little bits, but now, after ten years of study with her, they sometimes seemed within my grasp. At other times they vanished entirely, frightened away by the more prosaic demands of memory. Perhaps, in order to secure them, I needed to focus more single-mindedly on the piano.

'You very like me, and gifted at everything,' Mrs Sivan said. 'But these years *very* important for repertoire, and for absolute technical freedom. Very easy to say too early, too early, too early … and then suddenly too late.'

I was determined not to let that happen. Already I was

eighteen: it was time to get serious. I had spent my first year at university enrolled in arts alongside music, but now I decided to drop out of arts. 'It's not as though you'll stop thinking,' my father reassured me.

Alongside my practice and studies, I was working as proofreader for the independent newspaper the *Adelaide Review*. Its editor, Christopher Pearson, had offered me the job after I won the Tennyson Medal. It seemed a glorious position, and I took a hygienic pleasure in scanning columns of copy, eliminating typos. Each month, I felt a renewed thrill at seeing my name in its inside cover, clothed in its distinctive Gaudy font – emblematic of adult sophistication – albeit in very small type. But now my literary leanings began to seem a liability. After the disgrace of the Young Performers audition, I nervously phoned Christopher and offered my resignation.

'Do you understand the implications of such a drastic act?'

I thought that I did: it was not just resignation from a proofreading job, but a taking of the vows, a renunciation of all other possible careers.

'I do.'

'In that case, far be it from me to stand in your feckless way.'

Like a recovering alcoholic, I instituted a set of stringent new rules: no reading before 5 p.m.; four hours' practice before lunch; two hours' practice in the afternoon. Every evening I went to the gym, where I had devised an elaborate routine to increase my stamina, mentally rehearsing my repertoire as I moved through repetitions.

I picked up a pile of competition brochures from the conservatorium, and brought them to Mrs Sivan. She leafed through them, dubiously. 'In Russia, you have to do competitions, and only. Very sad to say, but very sport in music. Prizes desperately important: you could see it in our eyes, when they tell results. If no prize, they will kill you.'

'Really?'

'Of course not kill you, but end your career. Altogether, competition very dangerous for other reasons. Is *incubator* for mass-production musician. Can create you only to please people. I for life, I for health – mental, physical and emotional – and I will always fight for it. I develop people in harmony, in balance!'

'The Sydney Performing Arts Challenge is more like a festival than a competition,' I ventured. 'And it's held in the Sydney Opera House.'

'And politics everywhere. First, competitions were not corrupt, but now they come to business. And even if you win first prize, so what? People go to concert with expectation to hear circus animal, and not you as artist.' She took my hand. 'For you I want opposite. Must be individual. You don't need to please competition judges – not! You need only please the essence. How is Beethoven sonata?'

'Great.'

'Of course. You will do beautiful. Always remember, Beethoven very idealistic. Impossible really to be cynical person and musician – you will lose any ability to create sounds. And must learn Beethoven Third Concerto immediately. Very dramatic, very orchestral, very Beethoven. You will like.'

'Should I enter that in the Adelaide Eisteddfod concerto competition?'

She shrugged. 'Of course we can do competition *by the way.*

But aim not to please. Must remember, music is only person –
yes, exactly, I said *person* – you need to please.'

At home, I worked hard on Beethoven's Third Piano Concerto and 'Waldstein' Sonata. After a couple of hours spent
with his intensity, I felt sapped and emotionally fragile.
'Beethoven was eating himself inside out, was man who could
never find peace, *ever*,' she had told me. 'This is type of character.' I sat at the kitchen bench, refuelling myself with cups of
tea, studiously not reading the newspaper, when my father
approached with his car keys. 'Sweetie, we're just going to tennis, and we thought you could pick up Sach from art class.'

It was not the first time he had tried to coax me back into
the car, but this time I flung his keys back at him: 'I *told* you, I
don't drive!'

He gave me a sneaky look. 'Is it that time of the month?'

'What? Men have legitimate grievances but women have
hormones?'

'You have to admit you're a little irritable.'

'For your information, *I have been practising Beethoven!*' On
that note, I stormed back to the music room and addressed
myself once more to the beginning of the 'Waldstein' Sonata.

'Not,' Mrs Sivan said at my next lesson. 'This is orchestra
here. This is *pianissimo* of hundred people. More volume,
more distance, more abstract. Timbre is vital important to
Beethoven, because his voice is instrument, and instrument is
timbre. Timbre for him is his own sort of theatre.' I tried to
imagine a freighted *pianissimo*, with the weight and space of
an orchestra, exploding ten bars later into a *forte sforzando*.
'Exactly. And always steely fingers here, until suddenly we
come to church!' We arrived at the second theme of the first

movement. 'Clear chorale, and you can hear each – how do you say? – every *ray* of sound.'

Inspired by this analogy, I played the theme romantically.

'Not! You do like Chopin. Difference with Beethoven – more sustained, more masculine. This little bit – yes? – you hear it?'

'Yes.'

'Beethoven lyricism never just sweet. Must not beautify, ever. Like Mozart, Beethoven does not need your *make-up*.'

At home, I immersed myself in the practice of Beethoven, trying to probe his personality with my fingers, to feel out his naked, undecorated face. I searched for that little bit, for the particular flavour of his lyricism, a *dolce* that was sometimes noble and sometimes chivalrous, and never just sweet. But Beethoven did not surrender easily to knowledge, and instead seemed ever more full of contradictions.

'Beethoven had terrible – how do you say? – *people skills*, and preferred instruments to human beings. Constantly feel his social insecurity, and unacceptance. But at same time had *huge* love for idea of humanity. He's first who could support a revolution for brothership and friendship, without realising that any revolution comes in three parts. First, it's *idealistic*, second, it's *pragmatic*, and third, it's *criminal*.' She laughed sardonically. 'Beethoven enormous too honest man. This exactly in his sounds.'

The next month, I played the 'Waldstein' Sonata in the finals of the Australian Society of Keyboard Music Scholarship and was awarded first prize. Soon afterwards, I won the Adelaide Eisteddfod concerto competition, performing Beethoven's Third Piano Concerto accompanied by a second piano. I knew I did not have to please people, but it pleased me that I was pleasing them.

'Competitions can be killer,' she conceded, 'but can also be great great help. Can help your ability to communicate with audience from music. You want to go to Sydney for this Performing Arts Challenge? Of course – why not! But must learn not to depend on opinion, only learning from it.'

In July, as I boarded the plane to Sydney, I felt awestruck by the jet-setting proportions of my new life, by its national reach. But after catching the train to Circular Quay, I walked along the lower concourse to the opera house and began to feel anxious. Would I prefer to play well and lose, or play badly and win? Would it be better to please the essence, as Mrs Sivan said, or the adjudicator? As I pondered this, I came to a wide column, which seemed like a fork in the road. To pass on the left or the right? I paused in front of the column, waiting for inspiration, for my *inner hearing* to tell me what to do. My fellow contestants hurried past; a Japanese tourist took a photo as I pretended to be engaged in a study of this fascinating work of architecture.

Despite my slow progress, I arrived early enough at the recital room to hear several of my competitors in the Open Bach. The standard was much higher than in Adelaide, and when it was my turn to play I felt intimidated, and Bach's peace was elusive. I tried instead for something cheaper: a simu-lacrum of grace, swooning through the fugue, beautifying it with make-up.

Afterwards, I rushed from the room, disgusted with my-self, and climbed the steps to the top of the opera house, where I assumed a tragic, windswept pose. I knew I had not pleased the music, and surely would not have pleased the adjudicator either. As the afternoon darkened, I stared across the water. The buildings were outlined in black against a Technicolor sky; ferries careened in the harbour. It seemed as innocent and unreal as a child's colouring-in book: oh, to have the simple, honest life of a ferry! Slowly, the bridge turned into a silhouette and fairy lights traced out the far side of the harbour, and it was time to return to the recital room.

Surrounded by the other competitors as the adjudicator read out her comments, I remembered my dilemma: would I prefer to play well, and lose, or to play badly, and win? I admitted the answer to myself: I could beg forgiveness from the music later on.

The following day, when I arrived for the Open Beethoven, I was determined to redeem myself. This time, I would not aim to please the woman in the cardigan, sitting at the adjudicator's desk; I would aim only to please the essence. In my last lesson with Mrs Sivan, we had worked on the final *rondo* movement of the 'Waldstein' Sonata: 'It's like a dawn,' she had said.

Now, the first C-minor episode jolted the universe sideways, somehow, and changed my access to things, so that when the theme returned, the room filled with the white light of C major. I felt the relief of speaking truthfully: there was no place for cheap tricks under this brilliant light.

Back in Adelaide, the *Advertiser* ran a small piece on my achievement: *Young Adelaide pianist travels to Sydney and wins two gold medals!* 'Goldsworthy says she travelled to Sydney in search of greater competition,' it said, beside a thoughtful, questing photo. I tore the article out and pasted it in my scrapbook, where I was constructing a narrative of my life as a trajectory of triumphs, each larger than the last. There was no room in this story for artistic compromise, or for preposterous insanity. 'You're only as good as your last performance,' I reminded myself, and the bright light of that Beethoven had banished all previous failures into the past. Now all I needed to do was find a willing orchestra, and the first volume of my story would be complete.

Chapter 14. Shostakovich

AT THE END OF THAT YEAR, I picked up a brochure for Youth Music Australia's Summer Academy, held in Melbourne, in which members of the Berlin Philharmonic Orchestra would coach a select group of young chamber musicians. Although I had frequently accompanied my brother on clarinet, my chamber music experience was limited to the occasional flute trio with Helen and Monica, in which our chief concern was sounding good individually. In my accompanying course, the instructor frequently spoke of chamber music as being the highest order of music, but I suspected that this was a beat-up. Surely chamber music was what you settled for if you did not make it as a soloist: a semi-respectable refuge for the second-rate.

'Of course you must apply for this course,' Mrs Sivan said, when I brought her the brochure. 'Chamber vital important, and altogether you must learn from everyone.'

'It means I'll miss out on our family holiday.'

'Your family loves you. They will understand. In Leningrad, my whole summer was spent working for *zero* at ballet, to watch Nureyev and Baryshnikov, to give me understanding of choreography at piano. I learned enormous from this.'

'Really?'

'Of course. I begged them to let me have job. I told them *I dream of music, music is my life, I will do anything – I will clean!* And finally they came to depend on me. This must be your motto too: learn from everybody, always. And this academy great opportunity. From violinists you can learn phrasing, string sounds, sound production, bowing, imagination and fantasy.'

And so, on Boxing Day, as my family packed the car for Kangaroo Island, I flew to Melbourne with a handful of Adelaide musicians, including Helen and Leah. When we arrived at the university, we were assigned groups and repertoire, and I found myself in a piano quartet, playing Mozart.

'What is the meaning of this rest?' our instructor asked. 'Suspense. Expectation. You must not break this rest until the moment it is absolutely necessary to do so. And if you trust yourselves you will all feel that moment together.'

As we repeated that passage, he massaged my shoulders and trailed a finger up my neck, so he must have respected my playing. On the last night of the course, the tutors took to the stage to perform the Schumann Piano Quintet. Although they had not rehearsed, it was a piece they knew intimately, and the ease and fondness with which they played, gazing into each other's eyes, living in each other's sounds, was a revelation. The pianist stepped in and out of the spotlight: now soliloquist, now Greek chorus, now serenader of the violin, now lover of the cello. For the first time I understood the role of the piano in chamber music – its nimble dance – and I felt restless to join in.

Back in Adelaide, Helen, Leah and I decided to form our

own trio. 'Is fantastic idea,' Mrs Sivan agreed. 'Chamber music vital important. But first have to understand what is it ensemble. Two things: vertical and horizontal. You live your own life: horizontal, yes? But altogether terribly important to live together in vertical. For example, you, Mum, Dad, Daniel and Sacha – very different, yes? And yet living together in vertical, one happy family!'

'Sort of.'

'Exactly! This is secret of polyphonism, and ensemble!'

In our first rehearsals, held in my music room, my new trio was not yet one happy family. We read through the Mendelssohn D minor like three concerto soloists, each more concerned with the horizontal than the vertical. I had prepared my own part thoroughly, and when we finished the first movement, I sat back modestly, waiting for the congratulations. Instead, Helen came over to the piano and leant over my shoulder with her bow.

'There was a wrong note, let me see …' She tapped on a passage in my score. 'Here!'

I bristled. 'It's just that I have so many notes in my part compared to the strings.'

'No offence. I just want us to play as well as we can.' She returned to her seat.

We began again, and I kept my eyes fixed unforgivingly on Helen's violin part, until I caught her out on a faulty rhythm, and stopped to point it out.

'Can we please not stop all the time?' Leah asked. 'I just want to play.'

After our rehearsals, we sat out on the back deck, drinking sauvignon blanc, trying to decide on a name.

'We haven't considered flowers,' I suggested.

'Marigold,' Helen began. 'Daffodil, poppy, oleander. Chrysanthemum?'

Leah screwed up her nose. 'Too girly.'

'What about South Australian tourist destinations?'

'The Festival Centre,' Helen tried. 'The Rotunda.'

'I'm sorry, but I'm not going to be in any Rotunda Trio,' Leah protested.

My father brought out another bottle of wine. 'What you girls need is an angle. Something like Trio Stiletto. It's got sex appeal. You could all wear stilettos onstage.'

I rolled my eyes at the girls. 'I can't fit my legs under the piano in stilettos.'

'Even better: kick them off and play in bare feet! Put one on the piano. It could become your trademark!'

'Thanks for the suggestions Dad, but we're serious musicians.'

Alongside the Mendelssohn D minor, we worked on the Shostakovich trio. I brought my piano part to a lesson with Mrs Sivan.

'Who is Shostakovich?' she asked.

'The epitome of dignity,' I remembered.

'Exactly. But to survive this cat and mouse game with Stalin, you think you would be very open?'

'No.'

'Of course not. But Shostakovich didn't lose his dignity even *little*. Maybe lost in some ways his trust to people, but was still epitome of culture. Was epitome of everything.'

She opened to the first page of the trio. 'For example, in

this beginning, we have three voices, but *opposite* of polyphonism in Bach. Bach brings full peace of contact, of surroundings, of support, of communications, and of respect. This is his experience of life. But Shostakovich's experience different. What is to live in community, in hundreds, in thousands, and be completely lonely? What is it to have never ever chance to have consonance?'

She played me the opening cello solo on the piano, so that it really did sound like cello harmonics, with an eerie, glassy sound, and then the violin part, *con sordino*. Inspired by the parallel existences of these sounds, I joined the texture with my piano entry, in its growling bass, *pianissimo tenuto*.

'Exactly! This is full perspective of the sound! Of course, depends on one very small word: *if*. If these girls can do it.' She laughed. 'All life depends on this one small word.'

'They're very good.'

'Yes, but sometimes people *very good* at doing very shallow, very superficial. For example they take shell, and forget about oyster! We need to feed every time when we play, and not just polish the shell.' She took my hands and addressed me gravely. 'I tell you, music is not profession basically. On a very high level is way of living, way of breathing, way of acceptance. You see the world differently. Some professional people *doing* their job. They come to work and leave their coat on a shelf, and after put on and back to life. For us completely different. We need to *live* our job.' She glanced out of the window, considering something. 'Bring these girls to me.'

'Are you sure?'

'Of course I cannot teach *how* to play violin and cello. But what I can demand is respect to composer's intentions, and

understanding questions: *why* and *what*. It's terribly important they understand that arts started from arts. Aim always
is arts.'

I didn't know if Helen and Leah understood that arts started
from arts, or if they considered music a way of breathing; I
had never asked them why they were musicians. It was a question that seemed too intimate; it was easier to gossip about the
people we knew, or try to come up with a name.

'What about Trio Cerberus?' I suggested.

Leah screwed up her nose. 'Makes us sound hideous. What
about Seraphim?'

I shook my head. 'Too girly.'

'We need a name by next week if we're going to apply for
the Barossa Festival Academy,' Helen pointed out.

'Do we really want people telling us what to do?' Leah
asked.

'It might be good,' I said. 'We do need to think about the
why, what and *how.* I was even thinking it could be helpful if
you guys came to one of my piano lessons.'

Leah shrugged. 'Sure. Now could we get back to the
Shostakovich?'

At the end of the first movement, I jumped in before
anyone else had a chance to speak. 'Our playing sounds
empty. As though we were more interested in the shell than
the oyster.'

'What?' asked Leah.

'You can be strange sometimes,' Helen said.

'At the beginning, for example. We have three voices,
but it's the opposite of polyphonism in Bach, because of

Shostakovich's different life experience. What is it to live in a
community of thousands and be completely lonely? What is it
never to have the chance of consonance?'

Leah yawned. 'Do we have to be so over-analytical? Can't
we just *feel* it?'

The following week, Helen drove us to Mrs Sivan's house,
with Leah's cello strapped in the front seat beside her. I sat in
the back, feeling apprehensive. 'To be musician you need to be
first of all personality in one and not in pieces,' Mrs Sivan had
told me, but how could I reconcile the worldly, ironic individual I pretended to be around my friends, with the true believer
I was in my lessons? What would the trio make of my rever-
ence, my gushing earnestness?

'All very welcome,' Mrs Sivan said, when we arrived. 'Please
come in. Make yourself comfortable.'

I guided Helen and Leah into the music room, where they
took out their stands and instruments and tuned up.

'We're going to play the Shostakovich trio,' Helen
announced.

'Of course.' Mrs Sivan winked at me. 'I think I know this
piece.' She sat down in her revolving chair and whizzed backwards into a corner of the room. 'Please.'

As Leah began the opening harmonics, I dared not look
at Mrs Sivan, but when we came to the end of the movement,
I turned hopefully to her corner, and was devastated by her
impassive face.

'Everything fantastic, great,' she said, with a shrug.
'One only person you forgot to invite to this party: Shostakovich. You missed his spirit, you missed his character and

his intention, you missed his logic, you missed his sense of isolation and his intellectualism.'

My heart pounded, and I waited for protests, but both Helen and Leah remained silent.

'You used motif of Shostakovich, but is not Shostakovich. Instead, you play yourselves.' She pushed off against the carpet, propelling her chair back to the side of the piano. 'For example, what is this beginning?' She turned to Leah. 'You play like beautiful melody, but this opening much darker, much more lonely, really. Shostakovich has only one way to escape, and is *inside of himself.* Learn not to listen to anything around otherwise you will be getting mad. *This* is beginning of this trio.'

Leah began her cello harmonics again, wandering alone in the stratosphere, and then Helen entered, more human, more fragile.

'Exactly!' she called out. 'Coming much better already! Must miss not one detail. But detail not enough – what next?'

'Translation,' I volunteered, like the teacher's pet.

'Exactly. And after translation, what?'

'Interpretation.'

'Of course. But interpretation comes *after* translation and not before. *I want, I feel this way* is not enough. Every your wish has to be justified, with full support. Remember always one thing: Bible Bible Bible. Who has ears? They hear. Who has eyes? To see. It's exactly music.' She turned to the second movement. 'For example, what is this *marcatissimo pesante?*'

'Extremely well-marked and heavy,' Helen said.

'Yes but what Shostakovich *mean* by this? Is *biting* sound, yes? Altogether insisting ...'

Helen launched into the second movement with an

intensity I had not heard before, and Leah matched it in her response. As we played, Mrs Sivan sat beside me, singing and conducting, conveying the music's charge through her voice, body language and presence, until its abrupt ending, when she jumped up from her chair. 'What *this* is music! And freedom – this freedom of your fantasy – coming only with the great science and analysis. And never on expense of it. Understand?'

'Yes,' Helen and Leah said, in unison.

'You think you can be born – just be born, like newborn baby – and have doctorate?'

They swivelled their heads toward me.

'No,' I answered.

'Of course not! Must be enormous job first.'

At the door, as we left, she grasped Helen and Leah's hands. 'What must we always be in our performance? Convincing. And one person you have to convince is yourself. If you absolutely believe to it, everybody will believe to you. But other very important person you need convince apart from yourself is the composer. Because you need to know that he will be happy with you too!'

She kissed us each goodbye, and we loaded the instruments into Helen's car. As we drove down to the corner, I dared not say anything, awaiting the trio's verdict, but there was silence. Helen kept her eyes fixed on the road ahead; Leah stared resolutely out of her side window. It was only when we got the traffic lights at Portrush Road that Leah spoke: 'There's something very special about that lady.'

'Amazing,' Helen agreed, and I felt exultant with love for both of them.

✳

At home, as we worked, I started to feel a joy in the collaboration. Something was happening between us in rehearsals: something more elevated than our non-musical conversations. As we played the Mendelssohn, I let go of the horizontal voice in my head and started instead to hear the vertical; it was an erasure of boundaries, a return to some larger common mind. At the reprise of the first movement, Helen brought the sound to such a place of stillness, and Leah's entry was so fragile and interior, that I had to coach myself to keep going and not stop in wonder. I realised there were lessons to be learned here, beyond the obvious ones of counting and ensemble and balance.

At the Spring Academy at the Barossa Festival we performed the Mendelssohn D-minor Trio. The first three movements went well, but it was the *finale* that terrified me. I had made Helen promise not to take it too fast, because of the piano's giant handfuls of semiquavers, but now, in performance, she continued to lean on the front end of the beat, and Leah went with her. At first I tried to restrain them both, but then, recklessly, I decided to succumb to their excitement and generate my own, until we were all at the limit of capacity, heading towards glory or disaster. We came to the final octave passage, in which Helen and Leah were frantic beside me, and my hands a blur on the keyboard, but we remained together to the end, and the audience met us with an ovation while the final chord still hung in the air. There was such plaintiveness in that call, in its acknowledgment of sated need; we stood to meet it, buffeted as though by a wind.

Back in Adelaide, we decided to organise an official debut. We booked Elder Hall and had posters printed with our photo.

Helen stood in the foreground, her come-hither eyes staring over a violin; I loomed behind her, under a sheaf of hair; Leah hovered in the background over her cello, staring dreamily at the viewer, her face soft and wistful.

I brought the poster to Mrs Sivan. 'Is beautiful, absolutely. Looks like angels, and Seraphim Trio is excellent name. Keep this trio – has enormous future. But quality must be guaranteed!'

As the concert approached, our rehearsals gave way to administration, and that quality became more difficult to guarantee.

'I'm still not convinced by the name,' Helen said, as we folded flyers into envelopes, addressing them to our pooled acquaintances.

'It's an excellent name,' I said.

She looked surprised. 'I thought you didn't like it either.'

We spent an afternoon in the city, fanning outwards from Rundle Street, distributing posters. Helen confessed that she had mistakenly stuck a poster on the door of the men's toilets at the Austral Hotel. There was an element of make-believe to the project, of playing at being grown-ups. But as the concert approached, the magnitude of the undertaking became clearer: there were press releases to be issued, floats to be collected, complimentary tickets to prepare.

'There's something about your intake of breath at that pick-up that's way too stressed-out,' Leah told Helen, as we rehearsed the Mozart C-major Trio. She snorted by way of demonstration; I laughed, treacherously. 'Do you have to sound like a bush pig?'

'I'm sorry not to be seductive enough,' Helen said, 'but it's been a busy day. I've picked up the wine for interval, organised a page-turner—'

I jumped in, before she could claim any more credit: 'I finished writing the program notes at 2 a.m., and sent out all the media releases.'

'What is this, a competition?' Leah asked.

On the night of the concert, we arrived backstage in our concert gowns. We had spent valuable rehearsal hours arguing over which colour to wear, and this was the best compromise we could reach: Leah in silver satin; Helen in turquoise taffeta; and me in green silk chiffon.

'We match in an abstract kind of way,' I said, as we stood in front of the mirror, looking dissonant.

Helen took out her violin and applied rosin to the bow.

'There's no need to be nervous,' I told her.

'I'm not nervous. I thought you were nervous at the Barossa.'

'I wasn't nervous. I was just hoping you wouldn't push the Mendelssohn too fast.'

As she warmed up, Leah took her cello out of its case and languidly tuned up, and soon the green room was cacophonous with their practice. This enraged me further. Since I had no piano backstage, the least they could do was not warm up either, out of solidarity. I took out my make-up bag and obsessively refined my eyeliner.

'We have to be careful not to look like painted old bags,' Leah offered, and the intercom rang and it was time to go on.

I had known Elder Hall since childhood, but each time I

stepped out, it was to a different audience, and thus a different room. This time, I had two companions beside me, in mismatched gowns. I performed a stately bow, Helen an authoritative nod, and Leah a seductive curtsey, and we sat down with our instruments and tuned up. We smiled faintly at each other, Helen gave an introductory sniff, and we launched into the Mozart. She was a good, clear leader, and our ensemble was exact, but before I had time to register this fact, she veered spectacularly out of tune. Clearly she was having some sort of breakdown, but I would not allow this: above all the show must go on. Perhaps the audience would not even notice. I clung to this faith, and continued playing, resolutely, until she put her violin down, and Leah also stopped and turned to me.

'It's no use, Anna,' Helen whispered. 'My E-string is broken.'

Fifteen seconds into our debut recital we were marooned in that dreaded, loaded silence of concert disaster, amplified by four hundred listeners. As Helen ran offstage, the percussion of her high heels rang into the hush, and a haze of murmuring began. I was not sure what our next move should be – perhaps I should make some sort of Churchillian speech? – so I looked to Leah for guidance, but she was hugging her cello, and seemed to disappear into its body. I angled myself a little to the left, staring at the back of the stage, so that I could not see the expectant, confused faces in the audience. If I truly concentrated, perhaps I could will myself back to the safety of my music room, alone with my grand piano.

When Helen returned, there was a round of encouraging applause. She sat down, and led us once again in the Mozart.

This time, our ensemble was less certain. A tenuous collective faith had been undermined. It was a faith as fragile as love; it balanced our faith in ourselves on our faith in each other, none of which now seemed reliable. Leah missed an entry in the recapitulation; I felt a flicker of annoyance and split a note; a bar later, Helen messed up a run, and I knew she was judging me too. As we clumsily made our way to the end of the Mozart, we were just three teenage girls in prom dresses, trying to play together, not altogether satisfactorily.

The applause evaporated even before we returned to the green room.

'I'm so sorry,' said Helen, 'I tried to keep playing on the A-string.'

'These things happen,' I said. 'The point is that we should have recovered.'

'Get it together, girls,' Leah said. 'The first person we have to convince is ourselves.'

We followed her back onto the stage, where she started the Mendelssohn more beautifully than I had ever heard her play before, and I surrounded her theme with my accompaniment, gratefully; this was no longer a competition, and any inspiration she could summon belonged to the group. At interval, our three sets of parents flocked backstage, ecstatic.

'The buzz out there is terrific!' my father said.

'There seems to be a buck's night in front of us,' my mother said, perplexed. 'Where have you been advertising?'

They returned to their seats, and the intercom rang again, and we stepped out to play the Shostakovich. Leah sounded her harmonics with unearthly precision, Helen's entry was human and vulnerable, and I experienced my bass entry as just another part of the sound, something that did not belong to me personally, but to the group. When we came to the cello and violin *pizzicatos* of the fourth movement, Helen and Leah delivered them relentlessly as machine-gun fire, generating more and more energy – until there was a sudden explosion. We stopped playing, shocked, and heard the delicate tinkle of a violin bridge ricocheting down the stage. Helen sat quietly for a moment, and then stood up with a large sigh and walked off. Leah and I glanced at each other, and then at our bewildered audience, and then retreated to the green room, where Helen was sitting on a chair with her head in her hands.

'Why?' she asked. 'Why, why, why?'

I hovered around her, making consoling noises. 'On the bright side, the Shostakovich was going well.'

We heard urgent footsteps on the stage – an aggrieved audience member demanding a refund? But it was Helen's sister, Nicki, at the green-room door, with the stage lights glowing behind her. She had arrived late at the concert after a rehearsal and held her own violin aloft in beautiful radiant silhouette. Helen hesitated, and then stepped up to take it, and led us back to the stage.

There was a loud round of encouraging applause as Helen sat down and indicated that we should begin the fourth movement. At first I kept a protective eye on her, trying to cradle her in my sound, but as she pushed Nicki's violin to its limits, I realised she did not need me to do that, and that music for her was indeed a way of living, a way of breathing, a way of acceptance. This time we made it through the *pizzicatos* to the giant climaxes that lay beyond, and I revelled in belonging to such an ensemble, in being vertical. As a pianist, sitting alone in my practice studio, I had lived the horizontal for too long; now, as we played this music of loneliness and disconnection, I had found a tribe.

Chapter 15. Khachaturian

As I approached the end of my degree, Mrs Sivan urged me to apply for postgraduate study overseas. The previous year, Kate Stevens had moved to Fort Worth, Texas, to study for a masters degree. Fort Worth was the host city of the Van Cliburn International Piano Competition, and of the Cliburn Institute, an associated summer school. According to Kate, it was a mecca of pianistic talent.

'Of course they enormous appreciate Kate,' Mrs Sivan told me. 'You must make audition tape immediately for Cliburn Institute. They will enormous appreciate you too. This I guarantee.'

I did as she suggested, and received a personal acceptance letter from the director, offering me a scholarship to the institute and inviting me to audition for a masters degree. 'Is excellent news!' Mrs Sivan said. 'I not say America has no problems. Sometimes business instead of music. But they understand levels, yes.' She stared out the window at the empty street. 'In some ways Australia sleeping beauty. But really has huge future – huge! You know I am *enormous* patriotic. I met so many talent here, but so many robbed from having it, because not given them education. You think I came here by accident? In some ways yes, but really not. On large scale, I not believe in accidents. Must mean something.' She turned to me and took my hand. 'My darling, you will learn from everything and everywhere, but you must promise you will return here and teach.'

Such talk made me uneasy. I had not even gone anywhere yet: it seemed too early to promise I would return. Instead, I took the bright orange score of the Khachaturian concerto out of my music satchel and placed it on the stand. I had once more made it through to the second round of the Young Performers Award; this year, I was determined to have two hundred per cent security, and not to be preposterous.

'We can arrange composers by time and category,' she said, 'to make little bit more discipline in our mind. But composers people, not monuments, they are alive! Khachaturian is basically contemporary of Shostakovich, yes, but both men *very* different. Khachaturian as man was very generous, kind. Much warmer, and completely open, but at same time much more simple than Shostakovich. Altogether, you can say not huge difference in age, but for me Khachaturian *always* looks younger. Maybe because he made yourself feel comfortable with his age.' She opened up the concerto. 'And all of this immediately in his music. This concerto completely alive, completely full of excitement of life. But also, enormous *exotic* sounds. Not Russian, not. Is *Armenian*. And his style is very percussive, yes, but very *colourful inside percussion*. More than colour: *spicy*. Khachaturian is like master chef, and knows exactly spices.' She demonstrated a piquant harmony. 'People think is one position of hands, but is millions! Because all ingredients here, in hands! Altogether, what is it rhythm?'

'Rhythm is life,' I quoted her.

'Of course, rhythm itself give you all storylines. But at same time, all integrated: rhythm is the melody, and harmony is the rhythm, and melody is the harmony. They absolutely working like heart, liver and brain. One damaged, and no life! What point in being proud of healthy liver, if already dead from heart attack?' She laughed. 'This music combination of incredible visions. I told: fantasy unlimited on piano. Just one important word: *if.*'

This time, I did all I could to shore up the uncertainty of that *if.* I rehearsed the concerto in my mind as I swam laps at the pool; I repeated its varied choreography until my hands knew every movement, away from the piano; I analysed each tasty chord, each zesty harmony; I studied the orchestral score, until I could flick through it in my mind, poring over the entries of the bass clarinet and flexatone.

'Comes much better,' Mrs Sivan said, in my last lesson before the audition. This time, as I played at the ABC, I heard no mutterings of 'preposterous'. The next day, when I returned home from the conservatorium on my bicycle, my father met me at the front gate: 'You received the most important phone message of your life today, Pie. You'll be playing with the Adelaide Symphony, a week after you get back from Texas!' My bike clattered to the ground, and I danced with him beside the roses.

❋

When I flew into Fort Worth for the summer school, a volunteer picked me up from the airport and drove me down its freeways, pointing out shopping malls of interest: 'Y'all have shopping malls in Australia?'

She deposited me at the university, where I unpacked my belongings and then set out on a walk. It was hotter outside than I expected, and I felt disoriented by the strangeness of everything: the dirty blue sky, the emptiness of the streets, the squirrels jerking up and down the trees. An endless succession of SUVs whooshed past, their drivers staring openly, astonished by the sight of a pedestrian. I soon lost track of where I had come from and climbed a hill to get my bearings, struggling up the curb in the absence of a footpath. At the top, a car pulled over, and a man in a cowboy hat wound down the window, flashing me a giant Roger Ramjet smile.

'Hiya there, sweetheart. What's your name?'

'Anna.'

'Ay-uh-na. That's a real pretty name.' As he rolled my name around his tongue, languidly, it did seem a real pretty name.

'Thank you.'

'Why don't you just climb on in here, honey, and I'll take you wherever you're fixin' to go.'

I had not believed people really spoke like this, and felt further disoriented. Perhaps this was not in fact the real world, but a movie set, where the usual rules of prudence no longer applied. 'I'm trying to find my way back to Texas Christian University, but I can't remember which direction it is.'

'Oh, Texas Christian University is miles away. It's well beyond them hills over yonder. Climb on in, honey, and I'll take you there.'

It looked roomy and comfortable in his car, and I could hear the air conditioning working hard. But his grin switched up to an extra level of wattage – *what big Texan teeth you have* – and the world swung around and realigned itself, and I remembered that the university was in the other direction entirely.

'Thank you, but I might keep walking.'

I pivoted around and walked briskly down the hill.

'Ay-uh-na!' he called after me. 'Come on now, Ay-uh-na, it ain't safe for you out there, on them roads.'

I walked faster, nervous of being lassoed, but when I turned around at the bottom of the hill, the cowboy had disappeared. Back at the university, I secured a practice room and worked on Khachaturian, and gradually found my way back to the known world.

Next morning, I sat onstage next to twenty other young pianists and waited for my turn to play, while the instructor regaled us with anecdotes and demonstrations. A Brazilian boy played a poetic Schubert; a Romanian girl played Scriabin; and finally it was my turn to play Liszt's *La Campanella*.

'What is the secret of these octaves at the end?' he asked. 'If it's difficult to do semiquavers, do quintuplets instead. Then, if it's difficult to do this, play groups of six. Or even – my favourite – eight.' He rattled off octuplets like machine-gun fire. 'Suddenly semiquavers are easy by comparison! No problem!'

At the reception afterwards, a man approached me with a notebook. 'I am Demetrios from Athens, attending the Cliburn Institute as an auditor. Congratulations on your performance. Now I must ask: what is your genetic heritage?'

'It's a little boring,' I apologised. 'Fifth-generation Australian.'

He took a stubby pencil from behind his ear and transcribed this carefully into his book, in meticulous Cyrillic letters. 'I believe you are the truest Celt present at this course. I make this observation based upon your eye colour, your hair colour and the distinctive toning of your skin.'

There was a visiting conductor from England, running frantically from one young woman to the next. I wondered whether he was wearing a toupee and accidentally caught his eye. He hurried over to me with the glass of wine I had just seen the Romanian girl reject. 'I'm so sorry to have missed hearing you this morning. I'm *particularly* interested in your playing. How did you find the masterclass?'

'Everything he said was excellent.'

'But?'

I was still trying to work out what I thought. The instructor was a brilliant pianist, who spoke about technique and tempo and preparation. But there had been no talk of choreography, no talk of embracing the piano, no talk of what the sounds told you after. It had not been quite the revelation I had anticipated. 'But it was very general. My teacher at home often speaks about the *little bits*.'

'That's the most specious thing I've ever heard,' he spat out, his neck suddenly tight with fury. 'That's exactly the provincial attitude that gives Australia a bad name.'

I was so astounded by his reaction that I did not know how to defend myself. One minute I had been making small talk with an over-friendly conductor, and the next minute I stood accused of provincialism, of little knowledge. In a flash, I saw who I was to him: some girl from the colonies, whose suburban piano teacher emphasised the importance of playing nicely, of being *musical*. He took a hasty swig of wine, and recomposed himself. 'You have such a beautiful neck, like a swan. I love a beautiful neck on a woman.'

I excused myself, and went to congratulate the Brazilian on his Schubert.

'And I enjoyed your Liszt very much,' he replied. 'You remind me of someone, actually. A student here, also from Australia. Kate Stevens.'

'We have the same teacher,' I told him, proudly.

Late the following night, after the evening's masterclasses, the university's piano faculty converged in the auditorium to hear my masters audition. *What must we always be in our performance? Convincing. And one person you have to convince is yourself. If you absolutely believe to it, everybody will believe to you.* As I played in that midnight auditorium, I felt the freedom of the foreigner. It was easier to play on this side of the world, where nothing seemed to count. Afterwards, I returned to a practice room to work on the Khachaturian concerto, and in the early hours of the morning, the director came and found me. He told me I had been accepted into the course, and that I would be offered a scholarship. Around us, other students practised Liszt and Balakirev, even at this hour. I knew it would be good for me to come here, but the only vista I saw opening before me was that of an endless freeway, punctuated by shopping malls.

He seemed to read my mind. 'Texas is not beautiful like Australia, but we work hard, and wait for the chance to go elsewhere. I will enter you in many competitions, and you have a bright future, but you must be serious. Now return home to Australia, and win this Young Performers Award.'

❋

Back in Adelaide, I had five days to recover from jetlag before the keyboard final. It was an exhausting schedule, but I had to get used to it if I was going to be serious. 'In Russia, we were trained to play at any time of day or night,' Mrs Sivan told me. 'They woke us at three in morning, at four, and we had to play immediately. In any situation, in any temperature, on any piano. Definitely we have guts, otherwise not survive!'

The previous Christmas, my parents had finally coaxed me back into a car with a joint Christmas present for me and my brother: a mustard-coloured 1972 Toyota Corolla. Now I backed it out of the driveway to go to my piano lesson, and the first movement of the Khachaturian concerto started up in my head. I turned left onto Prospect Road and drove down to Kintore Avenue, waiting for a gap in the traffic to turn right. There was a gap, and there was another, but I was distracted by the *strepitoso* octaves leading into the orchestra's *fortissimo* statement and missed both chances. All at once I heard a gigantic crash, and felt a familiar constriction around my chest, and found myself fifty metres up the road, gasping for air. I pushed open the door and stumbled out to the curb. Behind me, a man stepped out of the cab of a semi-trailer. 'Sorry, mate, I didn't see you there.' He came up to my car, gazed at it with giant dark eyes, and giggled. 'She's a goner, I reckon.'

He was right. It was the second car I had written off on the way to a piano lesson, but this time, I realised, it was not my fault, and I felt a belated outrage. 'You could have cost me my concerto debut!'

'What?'

'I'm meeting the Adelaide Symphony tomorrow!'

He shrugged. 'Chill out, mate. I said I was sorry.'

The police arrived and phoned my mother, who came running up the hill in her gardening clothes. 'My godfather, my godfather,' she repeated, as a policeman steered the flattened car around the corner and back into the driveway. She brought me inside, and took out her doctor's bag, and gave me a checkup with trembling fingers.

'I have to go to my lesson, Mum. I'm meeting the orchestra tomorrow.'

She made us both a cup of tea and gave me a Voltaren. Then she fetched an icepack from the freezer and drove me to Mrs Sivan's house, leaving a yellow post-it note on the squashed car in the driveway for my father: *Anna is OK. At piano lesson.*

When I woke the next morning, my neck was sore with whiplash, but at least my jetlag was receding. My mother drove me to the ABC for the moment I had been anticipating for years: my first meeting with an orchestra. The conductor, Sir William Southgate, invited me into Studio 520, and I stepped inside to see eighty musicians packed into the space: a marauding army of dazzling, varied weaponry. They gave me a round of applause, and I sat down at the piano, reassured. I knew this place, at least: these black hills and white valleys, this familiar topography.

Sir William lifted his arms and brought them down, and the orchestra's sound filled the air around me. I waited for my exact moment of entry, like a surfer assessing a wave, and then dived in and caught it. *Playing with good orchestra give you wings, is greatest freedom, greatest joy.* The orchestral sound vibrated up through the floor and into the piano itself; I met it with my own sound, and it was the most thrilling conversation I had known.

'Good,' said Sir William Southgate, when we came to the end. 'That's about what I hoped. Ladies and gentlemen, we'll now have a fifteen-minute break, and meet Anna again at the Adelaide Town Hall.'

Was that it? I could have kept playing all morning. From the first taste, playing the concerto was an addictive pleasure, the type of pleasure that recalibrated all the others.

At the dress rehearsal the following day, I left my father in the stalls to gauge the balance and climbed onto the stage. The piano was perched at the far right, with the orchestra crammed to its left. My fellow finalists were shadowy figures in the audience; an ABC engineer ran back and forth, adjusting microphone levels; a lighting technician experimented with different settings, so that my hands cast shadows on the keyboard that were now pink, now mauve, now beige. I glanced down at the eight-foot drop to my right and then quickly looked away. Peril was everywhere.

'Right,' said Sir William. 'Last concerto before lunch. Once through from the top, with no stopping.'

The orchestra sounded different in here: more brash and less forgiving. At my first entry, my sound lacked authority, but I coached myself back into a simulacrum of heroism. In the second movement, I started to get warm under the stage-lights. The piano stool was too low, or perhaps it was too high. My breathing felt forced, and I remembered the vice-like grip of the seatbelt on my torso. Whose hands were these, playing these chromatic chords beneath me? What made them think they knew what they were doing? I approached an extended sequence of chord clusters, a chromatic progression over a C-sharp pedal point. It was a sequence I could have played backwards, but I began to wonder if I really knew it, or if I had always just been lucky. What if that luck had now run out?

Some part of myself enjoyed this question. Some part of myself wanted to know what this would look like, broken. I imagined the feeling of skipping a bar, and it was like the visceral anticipation of toppling of a cliff, that rehearsal of disaster that is vertigo: I felt it as a plunge in my stomach. And no sooner had I imagined this, than my hands – deftly, naturally, as I had trained them – followed my imagination, and the world shifted sideways, revealing the chaos beneath.

Stay calm and you will find your way back in.

I was now playing handfuls of made-up chords, like a child banging deliriously on a keyboard, marking time before the next orchestral climax. These were not the spicy dissonances of Khachaturian's concerto, but others entirely. Sir William shot me an anxious look, and slowly, inexorably, like an oil tanker running aground, the orchestra registered its panic. Behind my dry-mouthed horror, I marvelled that something that could begin so small, as a tiny cognitive event – a doubt, a dare – could translate so quickly into a catastrophe: eighty musicians, beached in a musical no-man's land with their instruments. Sir William drew his hands together in an emphatic line, stopping proceedings. In the ensuing, endless silence, I seemed to occupy the bodies of everyone in that auditorium. I felt my father retreat inwards, seeking to disappear, beginning with the retraction of his upper and lower lips; I felt the sudden animation of my competitors, their heady cocktail of empathy and *Schadenfreude*; I felt a lumpen resentment in the orchestral musicians, a rumble in their stomachs, as lunchbreak receded; and I felt a new distrust in Sir William, an anxiety about keeping this good ship afloat with a suddenly unreliable first mate. The one body I could not afford to occupy at that moment was my own, paralysed under the stage-lights.

'It doesn't matter at all,' Sir William said. His voice squeaked pubescently. 'Once again ladies and gentlemen, from the letter K.'

This time there was no margin for error: one slip in a dress rehearsal might be partially forgiven, but two slips would be suicidal. I clung to those chord clusters as though for life, keeping them focussed in my mind, staying on this side of sense, of coherence, and I made it through. But I had lost my nerve, and throughout the third movement I followed the orchestra meekly, hoping the day would finish soon, or that I would at least vanish from it.

'How did it sound?' I asked my father on the way home in the car.

A pedestrian crossed the road in front of us. 'Out of the way, you fucking idiot!' he shouted. 'You stupid fucking moron! You total and utter fuckwit!'

We drove on in silence. 'How was the balance?' I tried again, when we came to the lights at Prospect Road.

'Fine, yes, good.' He took his hand off the gear stick and

clutched my arm, as though I were a brave child with a terminal illness. 'You will be doing more practice before tonight, won't you, Pie?'

When we arrived home, I called Mrs Sivan. 'Much better to have problem in rehearsal than in concert,' she assured me. 'You know I always superstitious. Bad rehearsal means good concert. Enjoy your life! And always remember: music is natural communication, in sound. It's language combined of your wisdom, of your generosity, of your fantasy, of your imagination, of your physical precision – yes? – and of your absolutely clear communication. My darling, you absolutely prepared. Concerto sounded excellent in lesson. Just excellent. How often do I say that?'

'Never.'

'Exactly.'

I felt reassured by her words and practised for an hour, then had a nap. When I awoke, the morning's errors were the errors of a previous self, for whom I would no longer be held accountable. After an early dinner, my father and siblings left for the finals, while my mother helped me get ready. We had spent weeks selecting the material for my gown, in an exact shade of red that would not be drained by the lights. Now she helped me climb into it, securing it to my bra straps, and fastened the black velvet choker she had made at the back of my neck. My aunt braided my hair into a coronet, and I put on my drop pearl earrings: a birthday present from my parents, designed by Mrs Sivan's husband, Isaac. As I stood in front of the mirror in this dazzling outfit, I realised I had transformed myself into something safe. It was an armour, a superhero's costume, in which anything was possible.

Backstage at the town hall, my mother escorted me to my dressing room. She kissed me goodbye, and I sat down at the upright piano and practised the chord sequence from the second movement.

Miss Goldsworthy, this is your ten-minute call.

I started, surprised that the walls of the dressing room could talk.

This is your ten-minute call to the stage.

I practised the progression again, like a meditation, a mantra. In half an hour, this experience would be over, and I would probably still be alive, and so would my loved ones.

Miss Goldsworthy, this is your five-minute call to the stage. I repeat: this is your five-minute call.

But it was not enough just to endure this experience, to survive it. There were a thousand people out there, waiting to hear me! There was an orchestra of eighty, ready to accompany me! This was the fulfilment of my childhood dream, and it was only four minutes away. I realised my life had been building up to this moment, this grand Hollywood ending, in which I would triumph over all those obstacles, all those naysayers, all those doubts. Those elusive honourable mentions! My eighth-grade examiner and his toad-like C! Mrs Sivan's early words: *Anna will never be a concert pianist!* – all disproved! Pimples! Obsessive-compulsive disorder! Aural hallucinations! – vanquished without exception! Cowboy abductors! Libidinous conductors! Stoned truck-drivers! Even these could not stand in my way, as I moved towards this culminating triumph.

There was a knock on my door. It was Sir William, in a tuxedo.

'You look dazzling,' he said. 'I do believe they're ready for you.' He offered me his arm, and escorted me through the banquet room and up the steps to the back of the stage. I fixed a smile on my face, and as soon as I stepped out on the stage, it became genuine.

A honey-coloured warmth pours up from the audience, and this giant auditorium feels life-sized, the size of a room in my house. I sit at the piano, with its familiar grin, and nod at Sir William and the orchestra begins. From the moment of my first entry, I know I can occupy this entire space with my sound. I am a giant up here, controlling these eighty people to my left, seducing these thousand people to my right. The dress circle is close as a mantelpiece; the chandeliers hang like grapes, an arm's-length away. Later tonight, I will be summoned back to the stage with my fellow finalists for the announcement of results. Two of them are child prodigies; the other is half my height. *Very embarrassing, you looked like queen in kindergarten*, Mrs Sivan will say. *As soon as I heard ten-year-old play Liszt concerto I knew we had no chance.* Four months later, after winning the Adelaide Chamber Orchestra Concerto Competition, I will again be on this stage, playing a Beethoven concerto, and the conductor will succumb to heatstroke, and my parents will administer first aid to him, backstage. And three months after that, I will be on a plane, flying to Texas, the engines still resonating with my mother's elemental bellow, her animal grief, as I left and walked through that boarding gate and out of my childhood. I will feel as light as air up there, almost non-existent. But right now, I know exactly where I am. There is the X-axis of my life, lined up across the front row of the dress circle: my mother, my father, my grandparents, my handsome siblings. And there is my Y-axis, Mrs Sivan, sitting in the stalls, alongside her husband. I am held by their love, and I am held by this orchestra, and I fly through this hall in music, playing the soundtrack of my joy, my triumph.

CODA

Chapter 16. Mozart

A PHONE CALL FROM my father when I return home from trio practice.

'I've just spoken to her doctor, Pie. It's not looking good. You better get on that plane after all. Preferably tonight.'

'What do you mean it's not looking good?'

'I mean she's got a twenty-five per cent chance of getting through the night.'

When I hang up, the world is blurry, and I no longer understand the laws of probability. What does it mean to have a twenty-five per cent chance? *One hundred per cent security not enough: onstage must be two hundred per cent at least.*

'I'm coming with you,' Nicholas says, and he calls Qantas and books our tickets, and then I ring Helen and Tim. We are leaving for a competition in Italy in ten days, and our Mozart trio is still not ready. It lacks vocal hearing and pearly legato; the more we rehearse it, the more anxious it sounds. But none of that is important.

On the plane, Melbourne contracts below us, and I leave

my hand in Nicholas's safe grasp and close my eyes. I remember the first time I seemed to lose her in my life, when I had moved to America. The dazzling blankness of the piano keyboard, without her there to explain the why, what and how. And at the same time, a delinquent thought: perhaps I no longer had to *listen inside*, but could just decorate and inform and demonstrate and no-one would hold me accountable.

'Chicken or lamb?' asks the air hostess.

'We're not hungry,' Nicholas says.

Each night I had practised late at the university in Texas, in the small cell of a practice room. On either side of me, students thundered through Brahms concertos, until I realised there would always be others who could decorate and demonstrate better than I. For my first lessons with my new professor, I only brought repertoire I had already worked on with her, repertoire that she had explained to me. 'I know what you're doing,' he said finally, his patience expired, and I had to set off alone. Except that I was not alone.

'Could you please get us a blanket?' Nicholas asks the hostess. 'She's shivering.'

In Texas, my gifted housemate had invited me into her practice studio and had played me a Mozart concerto, and a parallel version had unfurled in my imagination, with a little bit more light in the sound, a little bit more comedy, a little bit more joy and conversation and theatre. *Mozart is like Midas. Every sound he touches turns into song.* 'How can you hear this?' my housemate asked. *What is intuition? Knowledge that has come inside.*

When I open my eyes, the world is once more a blur.

Two months ago I had a solo recital at Elder Hall. Afterwards, I scanned the line of well-wishers at the green-room door, but she was not there. I panicked: had I disappointed her? Debra took me aside. 'She went into hospital last night, but she didn't want you to worry before you played.'

My mother drove me to the hospital immediately; I was still in my concert gown, clutching my bouquet. She was propped up in bed, looking pale, but her eyes were lively. 'Would be exaggeration to say my health is excellent. But what you expect? I was child of siege of Leningrad.' She took my hand. 'My darling, Debra called already. Told that recital was beautiful, absolute.'

'You would have been proud, Eleonora,' my mother said.

'Of course. I very proud of my girls. Always coming more artistic, more mature. I told: real talented people always learn-ing. Open-minded is the first sign of talent, and then all life like magic door opening.' She leant forward on her bed, im-perilling her drip. 'Altogether, what is it arts? In big sense, it is unlimited flying of imagination. Not walk. *Flying* of imagina-tion. Unlimited fantasy, but in bracket of full understanding. And what is important in any arts? Despite everything you can say, arts has to be aesthetically and ethically grounded. Has to be foundation of beauty. Is *very* important. Beauty is a winner, because beauty is anchor of the life, beauty is founda-tion of the life, beauty is expectation of the life, and beauty is giving life. I don't mean beauty in sense of pretty face, but beauty as love and giving. And most terrible thing is a lot of people don't understand this. They understand love and giv-ing like duty words, like something to say in church some-times, and forget every day.'

'That's a good point,' my mother said.

'Please, my darling, tell me everything. First, how was Liszt? Good, yes? Altogether, looks beautiful, this dress very suit you. But still I prefer you with lighter hair, especially on such tall girl. *Much* more youthful.'

I had returned to my life in Melbourne, confident that she was getting better.

Now my father picks us up from the airport, and takes us to the hospital. 'Visiting hours are over, but I think you should see her.'

Nicholas waits in the anteroom, while my father buzzes us into intensive care and guides me into this underwater world. Schools of nurses hurry past, hushed with industry; my own unaided breath resonates in my ears. My father puts his arm around me. 'The first time you see someone in a coma, it can be a shock.'

When they wheel her past, it takes me a moment to recognise her. She is all absence: her closed eyes are oblivious as a newborn's; her hands lie mute at her sides. But I take one of those hands in mine, and feel that it is warm, and tell her that I love her, and then they wheel her through a pair of swinging doors, and she is gone.

In bed that night, I start to cry and find I cannot stop, even when Nicholas smothers me in his arms. I pull myself free and go to the lounge room, where my mother is watching television, alone. When I was a child, it was enough to go to her, and blurt out my latest horror – *rigor mortis* – and she would fold me into her warm living arms, and they would repudiate it. But even her arms cannot fix this.

Back in the bedroom, Nicholas has turned on the light.

'She can't go,' I tell him. 'She has too much to give.'

He brushes the hair out of my eyes. 'From what you've told me, this knowledge will have its own life.'

I think of the students she has animated with music, all over the world, and realise that he is right. But this is not enough of a consolation. My grief is more selfish than that. It is not only about her legacy. It is that she is my great friend as well as my teacher, and I am not ready for her to be missing from my life.

Later, he sleeps, but I remain awake, as though my wakefulness will keep vigil over her, as though each flickering digit on the clock radio's face marks an increase of that twenty-five per cent. Obsessively, I practise my Mozart trio in my head, seeking her sounds in my imagination: perhaps this too will keep her alive. At the end of *Maestro*, Paul visits the dying Keller in hospital and asks if he would like to hear some Mozart.

His eyes had closed – beyond music, it seemed. Once he had valued Mozart above all others: Mozart shines like the sun, he would murmur, his face tilting upwards, slightly, as if towards some imagined source of light and warmth …

I feel a suffocating panic: am I living my father's book? He cannibalised my childhood lessons; did he somehow script our future as well?

The following morning, she has survived another night, and her sister and nephew arrive from America. 'We have been through these sorts of emergencies before in my family,' says her nephew, 'and we have survived them. And I have no doubt that we will come through this one too.' He is handsome behind his jetlag, with lucid blue eyes, and I choose to believe him.

I return to the ward, wash my hands with antiseptic and take her swollen, silent hand in mine. *Hands can do anything. Hands can talk – of course! – can dance, can sing. Hands can fly – believe me, I have felt it!* Her teaching so transcends the physical that I have come to think of her hands as spiritual beings, and it shocks me, now, to feel the weight of this hand in mine. To acknowledge that it is flesh after all: an object, a thing.

Her student Gabriella arrives, resolute. 'There will be no grieving here,' she announces, 'only positive thoughts. I've seen people in comas before, and I can see from her face that she is fighting it.'

'Perhaps we should play her some music,' her daughter-in-law suggests. 'Do you have a recording of your last recital?'

I imagine a recording of my latest recital invading her dreams. 'I think the best music is in her head.'

Isaac comes in, with dark bags beneath his eyes. 'Great pianist, great artist, yes. But I don't care about this. I just want my wife.'

The next morning, there is a message on my mother's answering machine.

'Hello, Anna, it's Helen. I hope Eleonora is getting better. We're wondering when you're coming home, because we're supposed to be leaving for the competition in a week. Let us know what you want us to do.'

I press delete, and return to the hospital, where I sit by Eleonora's bed and wait for her, while Nicholas waits for me in the waiting room, while Helen and Tim wait for me in a practice studio at the ABC in Melbourne, trying to prepare for an international trio competition without a pianist.

There is a small square window at the back of the room, through which I can see a tree. A bird hops in and out of it, and I stare, disoriented. There is no redemptive message to be gleaned and no irony, only a bewildering dissonance, and around me the steady breath of her ventilator.

After the divorce, my mother sold the big house in Prospect. She moved my piano into the small front room of her new house, where it is tightly enclosed by four walls, like a beast in a cage. That night, when I return home from the hospital, I sit down and play Chopin's Nocturne op. 27, no. 2. It is a piece she has often played me. *I can change my interpretation a hundred times, depends on mood of day. Can be hopeful, like this, can be nostalgic, can be wise, can be more sustained, like this. Can have more space here, or suddenly more light, more freedom, younger even.* Tonight it is a prayer, and I feel a communion between my inner hearing and these sounds in the air around me. I hear every level, every line, every intention on every sound, and I realise that this is the place where she is definitely alive, and I feel this small room awash with grace.

The following morning, there is a message from Tim. 'Anna, we hope everything is okay. We're wondering what you want us to do.'

I know I am being unfair: the months of rehearsal; the tickets bought and paid for. She would surely want me to go with them. And yet how can I leave her?

'She could be unconscious for weeks,' my father says. 'But

every day it looks better.' He swallows uncomfortably. 'I think you should know. There's no guarantee that she won't be changed by this. Damaged, in some way.'

I return to her bedside and again take her hand. There is a needle taped into its back; an identification bracelet around her wrist. Where is she? I hope there is music there.

I was from absolutely atheistic background, completely. More than atheistic: communistic. A type of religious atheism! But I came to God through the music. Look at this beautiful world – all for nothing? We don't know what. But definitely, definitely something, otherwise this music not exist.

I speak to her about Chopin, and about our program for this competition, about Mozart and Beethoven and Shostakovich and Schubert. I speak to her about Tim's warmth and Helen's electricity, about my gifted students, about my doctoral thesis, about the generosity of my professor in Melbourne, and about Nicholas, whom I first met ten years ago at her place, when he brought his young cousin in for an audition. I speak to her about all the love that is crammed into that waiting room, waiting for her. It is selfish to ask for this, when she is fighting for her life, but I need a sign: I need to know that she will be coming back.

Basically, if you compare body and spirit, spirit unlimited. Body has a place, yes, body needs to be precise. Music has body too, but spirit of music unlimited.

Suddenly, almost imperceptibly, her hand squeezes mine. It is over in a moment, a wink – did I imagine this, to let myself off the hook? To make my decision easier? Perhaps, but I don't think so. I accept it as a gift, as an assurance and a blessing.

Three weeks later, in Italy, I hear her voice on the phone. She is hoarse and frail, but she is unmistakably her undamaged self.

'I was listening to Mozart. And *such* Mozart you would not believe. It was Mozart of the angels. The piano concertos, played so perfectly, it was *beyond*. I could see face of God in this sound.'

Chapter 17. Chopin

I HAVE KNOWN MANY other green rooms around the world, but this is my first green room, my Ur-green room. It is as familiar as a room in my house, as familiar as nervousness, and I might as well be that nine-year-old again, sitting in the third chair by the stage door, and then the second, and then the first.

Have I made it as I hoped I would?

There are six hundred people out there, waiting to hear me play, but this is Elder Hall, not Carnegie Hall. I have won some competitions and not others; I decided no longer to enter them well before I reached thirty. Like Paul, in *Maestro*, I teach piano at a university in Melbourne; unlike Paul, I do not feel disappointed by my life. I perform and record and make broadcasts; I spend a lot of time on aeroplanes. But a life in music no longer seems to be about 'making it'. Instead it is about living alongside these composers, getting to know them better year by year, about feeling out their private selves, like those of the other people in my life.

Which of those people are here tonight? I lean into the

stage door and listen, as if I could identify the audience from its hum. My mother and her partner are out there, and my father and his wife. My sister is probably in the dress circle, and Debra and Gabriella and their students, and both of my grandmothers, sitting towards the front. My brother is in London; Nicholas is in Melbourne; Eleonora is at home, waiting for my call. My grandfather is in his retirement home, recovering from an operation. I have been practising outside his bedroom this week, practising Chopin on his upright piano, on which so much Chopin has been played by both of us over the years. He lay in bed with the door open, while my grandmother tended to him and brought me mugs of Milo: 'Don't overdo it, dear. It's not only yourself you have to think about anymore.'

Tonight's recital is presented by Recitals Australia, formerly the Australian Society of Keyboard Music. Captain Frizzel has passed away, and Muriel Hopgood has retired, but the society still presents its subscription concerts in Elder Hall. I am playing a Chopin recital, built up around the great B-flat Minor Sonata.

This sonata basically Chopin's requiem for himself. First movement starts with grave, and after all story begins. Second movement is about dance of life, busy busy busy, like in enormous excitement and anxiety. This is scherzo *of life: joke in big sense. Why we have no time to sit down and listen, except when suddenly illness or something.*

My father was right: she was changed by her illness. She returned with a new serenity, a greater clarity. Her playing came back before she could properly walk again; her entire mechanism reconfigured itself around those hands.

And then comes third movement, funeral march. When you come through this music you will suddenly realise it's Chopin's own funeral, and he's watching to see how people will remember him. Middle section is so beautiful, so full of love, and so exquisite in nostalgia for life. He imagines how sad everybody be, missing great Chopin, and he suddenly feels very sorry for himself. It's very real, and very tragic, because he was living all the time under death sentence.

I have wondered if this is the music I should be playing for my unborn child, but it is all part of the *scherzo* of life, all part of what you are signing up for. I place my hand on my stomach and feel a reciprocal kick, and it is reassuring: I am not approaching the stage alone.

And then final movement – whoosh! Wind coming through you, in graveyard. It's not grief. It's beyond grief. This is how empty world is, when he imagines world without Chopin.

The intercom buzzes, and I pick up the phone: 'House lights are down. They're ready for you.'

I place the phone back in its cradle, and rest my hand again on my belly.

'Let me tell you a story,' I say, and we step out into the quiet.

Acknowledgments

I would like to thank my publisher, Chris Feik, for asking me to write this book, or something like it; for his patience during the long months of its gestation; and for being its gentle, expert midwife. It would not exist without him. Thank you to keen-eyed Denise O'Dea for fine-tuning; to Thomas Deverall for his elegant design; to Nina Kenwood for her enthusiastic support; and to the rest of the vibrant team at Black Inc. My dear friend and agent Clare Forster has been a constant source of largesse, providing everything from critical advice to baby walks and flying saucers. Thank you to my grandfather, Reuben, for his meticulous proofreading, and my father, Peter, for his editorial suggestions. I have quoted from his book *Maestro*, first published in 1999 and currently published by Harper Perennial. Many friends and family members generously shared their memories, and the recollections of Katrina Germein, Leah Jennings and my mother, Helen, were particularly helpful.

I would like to thank all of those who allowed me to write about them, particularly my family and Eleonora Sivan; writing this book, I was frequently overwhelmed by the privilege of my childhood.

Thank you to those who tended my other lives while I immersed myself in this book: Ronald and Margaret Farren-Price for inspiration and guidance; Stephen McIntyre for ideal neighbourliness; Damian Powell and Donna Davies for their support at Janet Clarke Hall; my siblings Alexandra and Daniel for their encouragement; and my dear colleagues Helen Ayres, Tim Nankervis and the indefatigable Helen Burbery. I would also like to thank Alberta and Mary Dowling for helping raise my baby and run my household, and my mother, who never once complained about commuting from Adelaide. Especially I would like to thank Nicholas Purcell, my first and ideal reader, for too many things to enumerate here.